Zareen's
Pakistani
Kitchen

Zareen's
PAKISTANI KITCHEN

RECIPES FROM A
WELL-FED CHILDHOOD

ZAREEN KHAN & UMAIR KHAN

Photography by Neetu Laddha

with Khaula Jamil | Cover art by Beygumbano

SASQUATCH BOOKS | SEATTLE

no wonder i am starving to fill up on this life. i have generations of bellies to eat for. the grandmothers must be howling with laughter

huddled around a mud stove in the afterlife

sipping on steaming glasses of milky masala chai

how wild it must be for them to see one of their own living so boldly.

—RUPI KAUR, *The Sun and Her Flowers*

To the generations of mothers and grandmothers who fed us with love.

Contents

Recipe List

WELCOME T

O ZAREEN'S

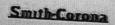

Dear Reader

This cookbook is a food crawl down memory lane, with easy-to-follow directions. It features the most popular dishes from Zareen's, our award-winning California-based restaurants, and our favorite homemade meals and street fare from our childhoods in Pakistan. We hope to share our knowledge, nostalgia, and the joy of great Pakistani food with you, the American home cook. The success of Zareen's restaurants lies in making Pakistani food accessible to American palates without compromising on authenticity. We hope to do the same with our cookbook.

Our motivations in writing this cookbook are threefold. First, we want to instruct home cooks toward a mastery of Pakistani cooking. Second, we want to share a nostalgic ode to the food of our childhoods. Third, we hope to inspire our readers to support our mission of women's empowerment, which is at the heart of our restaurant and all related endeavors.

SHARING OUR KNOWLEDGE

All cookbooks aim to teach. The good ones make the learning process undaunting. Given the perceived complexity of South Asian cooking, approachability was priority number one for us. So we shaped our recipes with easy-to-follow steps, generally available ingredients, and a close eye on preparation time. Having run

cooking classes and restaurants, we also thoroughly kitchen-tested our recipes so you won't find untested measurements that lead to underwhelming meals.

Given the incredible diversity of South Asian cooking, we curated our recipe selection to include the most popular dishes from thousands of Pakistani, Indian, and Bangladeshi specialties and staples. We chose some dishes American home cooks might already know from their favorite Indian and Pakistani restaurants. We also included some South Asian street foods that have become popular thanks to social media.

We hope you will find here authentic Pakistani recipes made accessible to American home cooks.

SHARING OUR NOSTALGIA

A good cookbook is more than a manual. Like any beloved book, it is a communion between writer and reader. Through evocative descriptions and photographs, we want to convey our passion for Pakistani cuisine to you. We want to share our nostalgia for the foods of our childhoods with all our readers: from the children of South Asian diaspora eager to learn the culinary heritage of their

parents and grandparents to American home cooks exploring the mouthwatering flavors of South Asian cooking.

Zareen's fan base is not restricted to South Asian foodies but spans *all* cultural, religious, and ethnic groups. We hope our cookbook is a trip down memory lane not just for South Asians, but for *all* our readers.

SHARING OUR MISSION

Finally, we want to give our readers a taste of our mission of supporting and celebrating women's empowerment. We see Zareen's restaurants as a vehicle for this mission. Our eclectic decor highlights trailblazing women: from our commissioned murals from local NorCal artists like Noopur Goel, to our featured artwork by Pakistani women artists and illustrators such as Shehzil Malik and Eemaan Bano a.k.a. Beygumbano, to our "wall of cartoons." And the majority of our giving is to women's charities in America, Asia, and Africa.

We see our cookbook as an essential extension of this mission. And so, interspersed among our own stories and recipes you'll find spotlights on a few remarkable women we love and admire.

In these spotlights, they share the stories of their work and impact, and name a favorite charity that we will support through this book:

Nadiya Hussain, chef, TV personality, author, and winner of *The Great British Bake Off* in 2015—Charity: WaterAid, UK

Sana Amanat, comic book editor and production executive at Marvel Studios—Charity: Palestinian Children's Relief Fund

Ayesha Chundrigar, animal activist and CEO of ACF Animal Rescue—Charity: ACF Animal Rescue, Pakistan

Michelle Tam, food activist and creator of Nom Nom Paleo—Charity: The Women's Building, San Francisco

Rupi Kaur, poet, artist, and author of *Milk and Honey* and *The Sun and Her Flowers*—Charity: Khalsa Aid, UK

Stacy Brown-Philpot, business leader and former CEO of TaskRabbit—Charity: Planned Parenthood, USA

We hope these stories inspire more women toward entrepreneurship and activism. And since we will donate half of our earnings from the sales of this cookbook to their chosen charities, you, dear reader, have our gratitude for supporting their causes and our mission.

Above all, we thank you for reading our work. It was pure joy to write this book for you—unaided by ghost writers human or virtual. We hope you and your loved ones find joy in these recipes from our well-fed childhoods.

In health,
Zareen Khan and Umair Khan

From Karachi with Love

An Accidental Chef's Journey from Burns Road to California Avenue

ZAREEN KHAN

My childhood home was a block away from Burns Road, the culinary heart of Karachi, and a few blocks from Urdu Bazaar, at the time its biggest book market and its literary heart. Back in the seventies, our Old Karachi neighborhood was more residential and tidier than it is today, but no less bustling. As a child, when I was not roaming its chaotic lanes with friends, I was at home reading quietly by myself. I was a biology geek. All I wanted to be when I grew up was a doctor. I was not interested in cooking.

Though being in the kitchen was not appealing, what came out of it was of supreme interest. I was a picky eater. I still am and would rather go hungry than eat something I did not find delicious. Thankfully, my Memon family—and my Gujrati father, in particular—had equally lofty standards. Food at home rarely disappointed: Memoni samosas, khowsay, Memoni daal, *dhokray* millet dumplings, chicken biryani, and all the take-away bounties of nearby Burns Road. And so I took my indifference for cooking and my love for its products into my teens, when two events changed my apathy toward kitchen craft.

There are foodies, there are Pakistani foodies, and then there are Pakistani foodies from Lahore. When my older sister married a Punjabi pilot, our family welcomed one of the latter species. Not only is my brother-in-law a Lahori foodie, he is a cook par excellence. The youngest of eleven children, Aitzaz Bhai had, from the age of four, assisted his mother at the

9

hearth of their rural home outside Lahore, helping cook daily feasts for a demanding household. When he cooked chicken pulao, Lahori cholay, and *paya* goat trotters soup for us, we realized what we Karachiwalas had been missing. My interest in stovetop sorcery was piqued; and once I started to seek apprenticeship to this art, I noticed the other sorcerers at home. I took in, for the first time, the talent of my mother, my sister, my aunts, and the labor and love behind my favorite foods.

My second culinary gain came when I stumbled into the cooking classes of Azra Syed, the matriarch of Pakistani culinary instructions. Well before cooking shows on Pakistani television sets, her pioneering in-person classes and popular cookbook taught my generation the art of Pakistani home cooking. Under her tutelage, I went from cooking and especially measuring by *andaaza* approximation or "feel" to precise recipes, a devotion to honing technique, and an obsession with quality and consistency. I, and countless other Pakistani women, were guided to our culinary success by Azra Syed.

Of course, I spent far more time at science classes than at cooking classes during high school. And there, at Amjad Sir's "O-level chemistry tuitions," is where I first met a boy named Umair. Teenage romance is all very well in Bollywood rom-coms, but Karachi in the eighties and conservative Memon parents make for a different reality. That, however, is a whole other book; here is the brief version of our seven-year journey from tuition center to *shaadi* center wedding hall. Umair's mother was the first to know about us and was very supportive. With her help, we gained my mother's and Umair's father's blessings in due course. Which left my father, a man who had always harbored deep misgivings of coed schools fearing precisely such outcomes. After some years of a Boston-Karachi long-distance courtship when Umair went off to college, we finally arranged for Umair's family to come to my home with a formal proposal for my hand. I served the customary tea and supposedly saw Umair for the first time as I handed him his cup of chai, under my father's approving gaze.

Shortly after marriage, I left Pakistan for the first time in my life to join Umair on the MIT campus in Boston. The vagaries of the F-4 "spouse of international student" visa meant I could not work or study in America. So I cooked. Umair and our fellow student friends were eager and happy subjects as I experimented on how to cook traditional Pakistani food on: 1) a married graduate-student budget and 2) without access to Pakistani ingredients and groceries—this was Boston in 1995 after all. Even after my visa situation changed, I started graduate school at Northeastern, and our eldest daughter, Samar, was born, the cooking improvisations continued. The most regular recipients of these experiments were our neighbors and dear friends, a Pakistani couple who babysat Samar while I was in class and who gratefully accepted Pakistani home cooking as a token of my gratitude. I see my time in Boston as phase one of my training in adapting Pakistani recipes to our American life, while keeping them authentic enough to please our Pakistani friends.

When we moved to California, cooking as a working mom of eventually three children gave me new awareness of the challenges of preparing food in quick time for picky eaters; all my children take after me in that regard. This was phase two of my training in making traditional Pakistani recipes more approachable time and effort wise.

A few years later I decided to leave the inflexibility of corporate America to spend more time with my kids. I soon realized this self-imposed work restriction, for someone who had always worked, was not a good idea. And so I turned once again to cooking, this time in the shape of Pakistani cooking classes that I hosted at home. Rave reviews for certain specialties, especially gola kababs and chapli kababs, sparked the idea of a frozen kabab delivery business. Curry Village Foods, the precursor of Zareen's restaurants, was born. With Paali, a cheerful, tireless Amritsari woman, as my sole helper and a small nook in a commercial kitchen as my entire domain, I was soon churning out hundreds of kababs, Umair and I delivering them out of our minivan to families in the Bay Area on weekends.

This rather unglamorous turn of affairs after a fairly successful corporate career and quite chic cooking classes did raise some eyebrows in our circle. All our friends—already addicted to my kababs—were unabashedly supportive. But some acquaintances were surprised and cynical. Spending sixteen hours elbow deep in gram flour and ground meat? Had I lost my mind? Had Umair lost his job? But the support of those who matter to you and to whom you matter is all one needs. And so hundreds of kababs became thousands of kababs a week and our poor Toyota Sienna crawled even more slowly up the San Francisco streets each weekend.

This was around the time Google and Facebook had started pampering employees with culinary excesses of Vegas proportions. Smaller start-ups that could not afford armies of private chefs instead hired caterers to provide free team meals. So I took the most popular items from our kabab delivery service and crafted healthy, flavorful menus for offices. The first lunches went to startups run by entrepreneur friends who were already fans of our kababs—a special shout-out to Aaref Hilaly and Zia Yusuf. Soon other startups joined, then came the venture capitalist firms that had invested in them, who in turn told their portfolio companies about us, and so on. In Silicon Valley terms, I had "product-market fit." And then I found out that I had cancer.

Amid the initial shock—the numbness, the consultations, the frantic online research—I kept working. The humdrum normalcy of chopping vegetables, making food, delivering orders, and getting paid kept life normal. Outside of the post-surgery recovery week, I did not stop working. I don't know which of the self-promises, epiphanies, changes, and lessons from

those weeks I have kept. I do know that I feel even more grateful for my work and more driven to do it well.

From our very first lunch catering, happily overfed tech workers had been asking: "Which restaurant did we cater from today?" I finally answered the question in March 2014 when I opened my first restaurant, Zareen's Mountain View, a small hole-in-the-wall right next to the main Google campus. Again, I chose what had worked best in the kabab delivery and lunch catering services. We kept the menu small and the decor bohemian, with a wall of hanging books and another for customers to write their comments. We were profitable in our second month, and I returned our family investment in this venture in eight months—a performance, Umair admits, none of his venture fund's portfolio companies are ever likely to achieve. Umair calls this progression from home cooking to cooking classes to frozen kabab delivery to office catering to the restaurant a perfect demonstration of the "lean startup method" and the "build-measure-learn" cycle. I was not aware of this as it was happening, but I am happy to be an entrepreneurial case study at UC Berkeley.

By late 2016, we were ready to open a second, larger location, this one on California Avenue in Palo Alto, near Stanford University. It was to be our final location, the one we would never outgrow. Within weeks we were inundated with long lines and no tables to spare. Zareen's Palo Alto was an overnight success, seven years in the making.

So we needed to expand again, choosing this time to go to nearby Redwood City. It was to be our first full build-out, a chance for me to design our restaurant experience from scratch. With Mountain View increasingly popular with Googlers, Palo Alto exploding thanks in no small part to Stanford students, and Redwood City in the offing, I felt we had truly hit product-market fit. And then we were all hit by Covid.

When offices shut down in March 2020, our revenues plummeted and the Redwood City project ground to a halt. I was not sure how or if we would survive. A few days after the shutdown, as we sat reviewing our expenses, applying for PPP loans, and figuring out how to keep our team intact, we started to see an unexpected source of daily revenue. Prior to Covid, we typically sold one or two $25 gift cards a week. We were suddenly selling about $600 worth of gift cards every single day. At first we had no idea what was happening. And then we realized it was the local community buying our gift cards just to support us and our staff. Many would come return their gift card unused. One loyal customer even approached me and asked if she could write out a check to me as a donation. Their love kept our staff working and our restaurant running. Amid the encircling gloom of Covid, they remained the kindly light that led us on. Karachi will always be my hometown. But Palo Alto is home.

So why do people love Zareen's so much? I don't know. I can only tell you what I love most about my work.

I love it when folks from back home feel proud of my success and see it as their success. I love that Pakistanis and Indians see our food as their food and host their non-Desi friends at our restaurant as they would at their home, mapping out their culture and cuisine on our naans and niharis.

I love when our food transports diners to the home-cooked meals of their childhood. Or when homesick international students feel at home again. I love to see people who have not grown up with our food fall in love with our dishes and become experts in and ambassadors of Pakistani food for their work colleagues and visiting family members.

Most of all, I love it when children of South Asian American families tell me how much they love the food at Zareen's and how its popularity among their American friends increases their own pride in their South Asian roots. I am blessed that all three of my children feel such a pride. My youngest daughter Amara was by my side when I started my cooking classes. And now my son, Sahlik, has chosen to be by my side to help grow Zareen's with me.

Finally, I love the shouts of "Gola kabab *para aquí*," "*La patrona no está feliz*," "*Tres naans, por favor*," and "*Rápido, rápido*" that ring regularly out of our kitchens. Pakistani cooking instructions delivered in another language and prepared by cooks from another food culture. And yet, nothing is lost in translation. Immigrants are the backbone of our restaurant and by extension of the community we serve. And as a fellow immigrant, I am very proud of the migrant mosaic at the heart of Zareen's.

As Zareen's has grown, so has my appetite to support initiatives that empower women. I was fortunate that my parents, like many Pakistani parents, supported their daughter's education. But there was much that I, as a young girl, was not allowed to do: 1) riding a bike around our neighborhood and 2) going abroad for college top, in that order, my list of "Off Limits Things I Regret the Most." And so, when you come to our restaurants, you will see artwork and murals and cartoons celebrating women's empowerment and showcasing the new generation of women and men championing education and economic power for women. Much of our impact giving is also aimed at women's charities in the United States, Pakistan, and elsewhere: Developments in Literacy DIL and The Citizens Foundation TCF schools in Pakistan, Heifer International, Planned Parenthood, and more. Indeed, this cookbook is an impact initiative in a small way. Half of the profits that we get from its sales will be donated to women-centric charities, and its sections are studded with our tributes to trailblazing women who have inspired me and who we hope will continue to inspire other women.

Recently a mother came up to me at the restaurant and told me that her daughter is inspired by "Zareen Aunty." By me, I thought: a girl from Burns Road who grew up on books, who was not interested in cooking, and who somehow is now the accidental chef marshaling eighty cooks to make thousands of naans, kababs, and mango lassis every week.

As I sat observing the lunch service at Zareen's that day, I recalled an afternoon when I was eight, sitting in our kitchen reading my treasured copy of *Tell Me Why*. My aunt, who was cooking, took a break from making rotis, looked across at me, and said, "*Itna kyun parhti hay? Baad mein to sirf khana hi banana hai.*": "Why do you read so much? All you will do afterward is cook." Aunts, it turns out, are always right.

Midnights in Karachi

A Food Crawl with a Returning Native

UMAIR KHAN

If you want to enjoy a mild London spring morning, a midsummer San Diego afternoon, and a crisp, autumnal Boston evening all in a single day, you will have to visit Karachi in December. And you should go there with a returning native like me who will pair these cloudless climes with the best kababs, kormas, haleems, halwas, naans, and parathas that rupee can buy. Our first glimpse of Karachi life will likely come as we sit in transit in the Dubai or Istanbul airport, awaiting the boarding call for Karachi. As we meal-plan our trip, we will overhear exclamations of "Waheed" and "Ghaffar," signs that the thoughts of the other returning natives are also running along the lines of famed kabab houses. Despite my many happy returns, I will still stand up excitedly the moment that boarding is announced, and it is time to go home.

With over 20 million souls to feed, Karachi is an untiring mother supervising some three thousand commercial kitchens, rarely sleeping before 3 a.m. In our food crawl we shall visit the best of these eateries and savor giant portions of delicacies that shall soon become obsessions. We will also meet some of the artisans, entrepreneurs, guides, and good samaritans that entertain, sustain, and ultimately save this ever burgeoning family.

The first meal of our trip will be the "full Pakistani breakfast" at Quetta Alamgir Hotel, home of the best lachha parathas in the nation. This being December, we will be joined by some of my Pakistani American friends, also home for winter. We will order a desi omelet each with extra green chili peppers, *cholay*, their famous parathas, and their equally famous, slow-brewed *doodh-patti chai*. The parathas are almost croissant-like in their buttery, flaky, multilayered thickness, and our initial request of two parathas per diner will prove insufficient. We shall need to order another round. Seeing some on a neighboring table, we will also ask for a few saucers of *Balai*—thick, fresh

cream that pairs well with lachha parathas. The bill will be shockingly small and our tip must be disproportionately generous.

Karachi is unlikely to win a "City of Parks" contest, even if competition is restricted to towns in the arctic tundra. But a mile away from the scene of our breakfast excesses is Hill Park. A poor cousin to the lush gardens of Lahore and the emerald hills that cradle Islamabad, its gentle inclines, well-maintained lake, play areas, and panoramic city views will, nevertheless, do nicely for a much needed sunny ramble. Located a few blocks away from where my grandparents lived, Hill Park was the one concession to nature that my city made to my childhood. Which is why I may wander off to find the concrete, spiral slide that was there when the park opened in 1967. It's comforting to find these nooks of Karachi unchanged even as the people around them vanish or wander afar.

Later that night our group of returning and resident Karachiites will head to Burns Road for Nihari, Pakistan's national dish (cue hostilities from the biryani camp). Burns Road is a few blocks of previously loved Victorian buildings. It is also the greatest food street in the world (cue hostilities from the Lahori camp). At Waheed Hotel, we shall eat far too much, and laugh no less at our gluttony. All of us will take a dozen "last bites" of dhaaga kababs and chicken boti's and nihari-soaked naans. One of us will inevitably ask our obliging waiter to run across the road to Karachi Haleem

and bring us a few plates of their famous Beef Haleem. When you exclaim at this multi-restaurant food service, we will reply: "*Yeh Karachi Hai, Meri Jaan*" This is Karachi, My Dear. There will be no room for Rabri, *the* decadently creamy dessert I have raved about all evening. So we shall walk over to Delhi Rabri House and buy some rabri to go, but end up eating it all in front of the bemused cashier. We will also get a few clay pots of Kheer to go, but they will be consumed before our car leaves the aging mansions of Old Karachi. All shall be miraculously calm the next morning, proving that God exists, is merciful, and loves Pakistani food.

Karachi is gilded with 30 miles of golden coastline, much of it dotted with rentable beach "huts"—well-appointed, spacious seaside houses. December in Karachi means a pilgrimage to such a hut, bathing in warm, calm waters, and eating biryani on the beach—the food of choice for group picnics. Karachi is embarrassingly rich in biryani choices: Nalli Marrow Biryani at Ghousia, Student Biryani, White Biryani, Madni Biryani, Farhan Biryani, Biryani of the Seas, the surprisingly good biryanis at its haleem houses, and the often superior biryanis of countless home kitchens. As our beach hut will come with a well-stocked kitchen and an entourage of domestic help, our home-made Memoni Chicken Biryani will be heated on site and steaming platefuls handed out at lunch time. Picking up seashells on the shores of the Arabian Sea with biryani-stained fingers should be on everyone's bucket list.

Part two of our seaside day shall start at dusk when we go "crabbing" after dark. Departing from the Port of Kemari, our four-hour night sail will take us out to one of the coastal islands such as Manora or Bhit Island. Here we will do some nighttime hunting for mud crabs using crab pots and gloved hands. On our return voyage, we will enjoy a late night seafood dinner cooked on our boat by our hospitable fishermen-chefs from their and our catches of the day.

This food crawl is also a work trip for me, and with the start of the work week, shall begin my daily visits to my work family at Folio3. But work lunches and office parties in Karachi are next level. There are spontaneous samosa-pakora-chai celebrations at work whenever rain cools off an afternoon in the eight-month-long summer. Then there are rooftop barbecue dinners with onsite tandoor ovens and charcoal pits spicing up balmy nights. There are "Mango Madness" fests during peak summer, featuring the very best of Pakistani mangoes, which are the very best mangoes in the world—ice buckets of Chownsa, Langra, and Anwar Ratool mangoes—sliced, diced, made into shakes, served as ice cream, or eaten with parathas.

You will miss out on these summery delights in December but to make up for it we will invite you to join us for a midday feast of Peshawari Dum Pukht: a whole marinated goat, stuffed with pulao and vegetables, slow cooked on a wood burning fire, served and eaten communally out of large

platters. In case you are wondering, work also does get done here at Folio3 and elsewhere in corporate Karachi.

The startup scene in Karachi is lit, and my weeknights will be taken over by hangouts with entrepreneurs. Many of these meetings are at trendy coffee hotspots so tag along to meet tech trailblazers and try out the new generation of Karachi cafés offering superb coffee, impeccable service, and bohemian decor usually featuring mini libraries and art galleries. A popular and less bougie venue for late night shop talk is Chotu Chaiwala. Many hours after dinner, we will go there to sit on brightly colored plastic chairs set in an abandoned parking lot. You will get to pick your paratha fillings: cheese, egg, potato, chicken, or Nutella. Then you shall pair the parathas with your choice of Zafrani Saffron Chai, Kashmiri Chai, or Doodh Patti Chai. Feeding on such high-octane fuel at midnight, inhaling the irrational optimism of startup founders, fanned by the breeze off the Arabian sea, you will achieve Peak Karachi, where everything is instantly possible.

Some of these founder meetups will likely happen at Sind Club, that well-manicured relic of Karachi's colonial past. Over 140 years old, it has aged well under the watchful care of anglophiliac "pukka sahibs." Despite its old world restrictions, its bistro is an inviting place for startup confabs, serving unexpectedly authentic aloo qeema and paratha. Karachi Gym- khana, the other grande dame of the city's country club roster, is a personal favorite, its sprawling lawns and pools having served as my childhood playground. We will make time for a late night, open-air barbecue on its verandahs—a long standing family tradition—to savor possibly the best charcoal-grilled chicken in town.

In time, our feasts of reason with tech entrepreneurs will make way for flows of soul with Karachi's impact entrepreneurs, each as resilient and resourceful as the city they care for.

First, we will visit Lyari, the once crime ridden slum that Kiran Foundation School has helped transform to a thriving neighborhood. Under the care of founder Sabina Khatri, simply known as *Maa* mother, Kiran school has given world-class education to children, sanctuary to victims of violence, resources to families, and hope to the community.

Across town we will meet with another remarkable woman, Ayesha Chundrigar. Her nonprofit "ACF—Animal Rescue" runs the largest street animal sanctuary in Pakistan and advocates for compassion, always, toward both the animals and humans of Karachi. More about her on page 165.

Our final stop will be Indus Hospital, a private nonprofit hospital providing free health care to all. Our host, Dr. Junaid Patel, a high school friend, will take time out to show us around the state-of-the-art facility, pointing out signs that proclaim it is illegal to ask anyone for fees and request patients to report any one who does so. Their visionary founder, Dr. Bari, and his team have grown a seemingly impossible social experiment into a healthcare system that each year serves 6 million patients who would otherwise go uncared for.

Traversing this mega city to meet all three Samaritans in a single day will likely leave no time for sit-down meals. But intermittent fasting is never part of a Karachi food crawl and we will pick up some of the most popular portable snacks: paratha rolls from Silver Spoon Restaurant off Tariq Road; savory chicken puff pastries from Blue Ribbon Bakery; Hanifia's Hunter Beef Burgers—the Pakistani take on pastrami; as well as the best snacks-on-wheels on offer by street hawkers: shakar-kandi baked sweet potato sprinkled with chaat masala and lemon; bhutta fire-roasted corn on the cob smeared with salt, chili pepper, and lemon; and gola gunda shaved ice cone drenched in multicolored syrups. That night we shall head to my favorite kabab house in all Karachi, Ghaffar's. Over some of the best gola kabab and nihari in the country, served on rickety roadside tables, we will raise our cans of Pakola Ice Cream Soda to the generous souls who are relentlessly saving Karachi from itself.

Having had our fill of tech and impact entrepreneurs, we shall let a different set of innovators take us back to full throttle food and city crawling. These are the young men and women conducting street food and city architecture tours, with "Super Savari Express" being the most popular of a diverse and growing pack. Your mode of transportation can

be a gaily painted bus, an upgraded rickshaw, or even a horse and carriage. The tours will show you the architectural prides of all Karachi-walla's as you sample some of the best street food on offer: cholay chaat, dahi baray, pani puri, bun kabab, kulfi—popsicle-stick, tall glasses of falooda, and of course cups upon cups of *Karak* strong *Chai*. You will visit Victorian-era landmarks such as Empress Market and Denso Hall; roam Frere Hall, a venetian-gothic limestone marvel, built originally as Karachi's City Hall; and explore Mohatta Palace and Museum, a piece of Rajasthan India in the heart of Karachi. These glimpses of Old Karachi are still eye-catching, some because of loving restoration, others despite benign neglect.

December is *shaadi* wedding season in Pakistan and so we must crash a wedding—best done through some officially invited kith or kin. The invitation will be for 9 p.m., we will show up at 10, the more hardened wedding goers will arrive at 11, and the food will be served shortly before midnight, allowing us to take in the costumery and pageantry of a Pakistani wedding at our leisure. Such delayed gratification shall heighten the pleasure of finally feasting on mutton korma, seekh kababs, karahi chicken, naans baked in onsite clay ovens, deep fried *jalaybees* freshly dunked in syrup, and pink Kashmiri chai. The host family, from grandchild to grandparent, will insist on feeding us well past breaking point, directing servers to bring fresh naans and hot kababs to our table, apologizing for the delays, and thanking us repeatedly for sharing in their joy. Only in Pakistan could uninvited guests be so unconditionally welcomed.

Our final weekend will start out with a Halwa Puri brunch at Fresco, a Karachi institution since 1952, with my Habib Public schoolmates. Besides their legendary Halwa-Puri, we also will sample many of their halwas and mithais— traditional Pakistani confections: *gulab jamun*, *motichoor laddu* (round balls of chickpea and sugar syrup), *burfi* and *kalakand* (cream and cheese based fudge-like desserts), *akhrot* (walnut halwa), *habshi* halwa (dark brown halwa made with wheat and almonds). A great many calories and carbs shall be enjoyed by all. The sugar high should help you indulge us middle-aged school kids our reunion conversation, which will veer from Burns Road to California Avenue, vacillate between our lives in the 1980s and in the 2020s, and eulogize teachers past and mates abroad. Only old school friends drifting away from their childhood island on separate rafts would find sense or succor in it.

The final day will likely be overrun with shopping for souvenirs and gifts, footwear and fashionwear Western and Eastern, flawless leather goods and near-perfect brand knockoffs. A hesitant bargainer like me is a liability on bazaar crawls and some of my more capable cousins and aunts will have to be sought out. In their company we will visit glitzy boutiques in Karachi's modern malls, the veteran shopkeepers of Tariq Road, and the bustling stalls and stores of Zainab Market and Bohri Bazaar. In the care of our experienced guides, the shopping options and stops will keep multiplying. My swooning spirits on this never-ending quest will rebound when our entourage reaches Nimco's, the final stop of all departing visitors to Karachi. Here we will acquire a garrison-feeding supply of traditional crunchy snacks: *Bhel Puri*, *Ghatia*, *Masala Papri*, *Spicy Peanuts*, *Chewra*, *Namak Paray*, and some thirty other Pakistani takes on the potato chip.

For our last supper in Karachi, we will head to The East End. The ethnic food that Zareen introduced me to in our first years together is reincarnated by the chef here. On offer are some of the greatest hits of Bohri, Memoni, and Parsi cuisine: Mutton Masala Chops, *Khattay Aloo tangy potatoes* , *Maal Puray* Gujarati pancakes served with rabri, succulent Kemari crabs, mutton roast with unctuous masala clinging onto tender meat, *Imli* tamarind shots, *Falsa* berry juice laced with black salt. The menu bookends traditional mains with modern, playful riffs on appetizers and desserts. The languid beauty of its old-school decor recalls the more innocent and elegant heydays of my city, preserving forever a past that never quite existed.

A food crawl across my hometown of Karachi ends up reminding me of my present home in California. Fresco's Halwa Puri reminds me of Zareen's weekend Halwa Puri platter. The East End dinner recalls the special nights she makes Memoni *Khowsay* and *Dhokray* millet dumplings in vegetable stew. And, of course, at the gate-crashed wedding my own bride was missing, missed out, and was missed. All these will leave me feeling a bit homesick. It is a fortunate migrant who makes such happy memories on new shores that it too becomes a home to yearn for and miss.

And so after prolonged Pakistani goodbyes, surprise parting gifts, urgings to stay in touch, promises to return, to visit, to meet again, on the stroke of our final Karachi midnight, we shall head back to the airport.

Like the siren call of slot machines at Las Vegas airport, the colors and aroma of the in-terminal Rehmet-e-Shereen store at Karachi Airport will lure us in for one last hit of mithai. At our gate we will open a tin of recently bought gulab jamuns and begin to plan our return trip to Pakistan. The sequel must cover Lahore, a food-lover's paradise and the jewel in the Mughal crown, as well as Northern Pakistan, an alpine paradise where reside the three tallest mountain ranges in the world: Himalaya, Karakoram, and Hindu-Kush.

We will wrap up our sequel planning and stand up excitedly the moment that boarding is announced, and it is time to go home.

The Desi Pantry

In this section we list the most commonly used ingredients, equipment, and techniques in the Desi, i.e., South Asian, kitchen and, therefore, in this book. We start with a few words on how to use this book, that is, how to interpret and apply our recipes.

ON USING THIS BOOK

ON RECIPE RATINGS: We have included a rating for all our recipes as Easy, Intermediate, or Advanced effort. This is an admittedly rough indicator of both the level of effort in terms of active cooking time and the level of expertise, skill, and experience with Pakistani cooking needed to make the dish. Most of our recipes (more than 50 percent) are Easy, and about 10 percent are Advanced.

ON VEGETARIAN AND VEGAN DISHES: All vegetarian dishes in this book are marked with a Ⓥ icon. If a dish is vegan, you will also see a Ⓥⓔ. Most Pakistani vegetarian dishes that are not vegan are easily made vegan by substituting oil for ghee/butter, coconut or oat milk for regular milk, and dairy-free vegan yogurt in place of whole milk yogurt.

ON MEASUREMENTS: All our measurements are subject to change—by you. You can try the recipe as is the first time and make it your own afterward. Some of you will find our recipes under spiced; others may find things a bit too hot to handle. Bottom line: all spices, especially cayenne, red chili powder, and green chilies, should be adjusted according to your taste, or treated as optional.

ON ALTERNATIVE INGREDIENTS: Never give up on a recipe just because an ingredient or two are missing from your pantry. We have made the less easily available ingredients optional and often suggest alternatives in the recipe. You can find substitutes for many spices and herbs in the ingredients section beginning on page 34.

ON CONSISTENCY OF STEWS AND CURRIES: The consistency of curries can range from light and thin to thick and gravy-like. On the one end is *saalan*, the name given to a runny "wet" curry, as in aloo gosht. On the other end is a richer "dry" curry called *korma*, as in the thick curry used in chicken biryani.

LENTILS / DAALS: These dishes also have different consistencies. A "dry" lentil is a lentil that is tenderized in water but served with essentially no sauce, and it's usually enjoyed with bread, rather than rice. "Wet" lentils, the more common type of daals, have a nice sauce, which itself can range from watery thin to Thanksgiving gravy thick. Depending on their consistency, wet daals may be enjoyed with rice, roti, or naan.

ON DEEP-FRYING: We assume a temperature of 350 degrees F for oil considered ready for deep-frying. If you don't have a food ther-mometer, do the wooden spoon test: Stick the end of a wooden spoon into the oil. If bubbles form around the wood and float up, your oil is ready for deep-frying.

ON GARNISHING: Pakistani cuisine offers a dizzying choice of garnishes: fresh chopped cilantro the most common savory topping, fresh chopped mint, sliced green chili peppers, slivered ginger, sliced green onions, lemon slices, and crisp-fried onions being the most popular. A sprinkle of garam masala over curries and of chaat masala over savory snacks is also customary. In sweet dishes, slivered or crushed nuts especially pistachios, almonds, or cashews, raisins, and saffron strands, are all popular garnishes. All of us Pakistani home cooks have our favorites that we overuse. In many of our recipes, we have limited the garnish choices or made them optional to reduce both confusion and extra effort with the notable and necessary exception of Memoni-Style Khowsay on (page 111). The choice of toppings is entirely yours.

ON HOMEMADE VS. STORE-BOUGHT ITEMS: Many of the chutneys, masalas, and breads in this book have convenient, fairly acceptable substitutes in Indian/Pakistani grocery stores.

CHUTNEYS: Our recipes for tamarind imli chutney and green hari chutney are simple enough that you should not need desi store-bought alternatives. But they are readily available when you are running short on ingredients and time. Try to find brands that go easy on preservatives and artificial colors. Neon green in chutney is not a thing.

GARAM MASALA AND CHAAT MASALA: Nothing store-bought will beat the aroma and flavor of homemade garam masala and chaat masala. But if you run out, you can always don dark sunglasses, a muffler, and a hat, and skulk into your local desi store to buy a back-up box of each. As with chutneys, look for spice mixes that are low on artificial additives.

NAANS: For good reason, naans are rarely made at home, except on very special occasions. So if you want to enjoy naans with any of our main dishes but without any of the labor, you have two easy choices: fully cooked, packaged naans as well as frozen naans are available in most South Asian grocery stores. Fresh-from-the-tandoori-oven naans, picked up from your favorite Indian or Pakistani restaurants, are the best if more expensive way to go. Naans keep well in the fridge and freezer. Simply toast them in your toaster or toaster oven, heat in a conventional oven, or pan fry in a little ghee or butter before serving.

PARATHAS: Parathas are far more commonly made at home than naans. But the convenience of getting frozen, ready-to-fry parathas from the store cannot be denied. Store-bought parathas free you up to focus on your fabulous, made-from-scratch fillings for your signature paratha rolls, and your guests are none the wiser. Simply pan fry store-bought parathas on a lightly greased skillet or *tava* at meal or party time. Likewise, uncooked and ready-to-deep-fry puris are now available at most South Asian stores.

INGREDIENTS

GHEE AND OILS: Ghee is clarified butter used for cooking. Made by slowly simmering butter and removing the milk solids, ghee has a higher smoke point than butter, making it ideal for shallow-frying and sautéing. Its silken texture lends depth and its golden color adds richness to all our favorite Pakistani dishes from biryanis to daals, to desserts. We love ghee and encourage others to fall in love with it too. But as it may be less available and more expensive, most of our recipes offer an option to use cooking oil. Butter is always an option too, but avoid it for deep-frying. In Pakistani cooking, oils with more neutral flavors are preferred. We recommend avocado oil for high-heat cooking and olive oil or avocado oil again for sautéing. For deep-frying, it's OK to use a less expensive vegetable oil.

MEAT / GOSHT CHOICES: Most Pakistani meat main dishes can be made with a variety of meats. Aloo Gosht (page 120), Aloo Qeema (page 121), biryani, and karahi are equally popular when made with chicken, lamb, mutton, or beef. Some specialties like nihari and haleem are best known as beef dishes, but even these have popular chicken and lamb versions. Much of the recipe remains largely unchanged across the different meats. This happy fact gives you at least three possible versions for nearly all meat recipes! Only the amount of cooking time and the amount of water needed to tenderize the meat varies. More time is needed for beef than for lamb/mutton, and even less for chicken. We note these potential substitutions in several recipes, but you should freely use this interchangeability when making any Pakistani meat recipe.

NUTS: Most Pakistani desserts and some savory dishes call for nuts—usually almonds, cashews, and pistachios—as ingredients or for garnish. In most cases these are optional and can be skipped, especially if nut allergies are a concern. Our recipes always assume raw, unsalted nuts, and we specify whether whole, chopped, or slivered forms are required.

SALT / NAMAK: Salt is *always* to taste: that is, the salt measurements in our recipes are simply our preference and meant as guidance. The amount of salt to use depends on a) the type of salt and b) how salty you like your food. We typically use sea salt for cooking at home, and recipes in this book were tested with sea salt for consistency. If you use pink Himalayan salt (fun fact: nearly all "pink salt" in the United States comes from Pakistan!), kosher salt, or iodized table salt, the salt measurements may need to be adjusted.

Spices, Essences, and Aromatics

BASIL SEEDS / TUKH MALANGA: These are the small, black seeds of the sweet basil plant. Similar to chia seeds, these seeds are often soaked in water, causing them to swell and develop a gelatinous outer layer. Basil seeds add a unique chewy texture and visual appeal to drinks and desserts. They are especially popular additions to falooda, a traditional Pakistani dessert beverage.

BLACK PEPPER / KALI MIRCH: Known for its pungent, spicy flavor and aroma, black pepper is widely used in Pakistani cuisine to enhance the flavor of savory dishes, sauces, and marinades. It comes from the dried berries of the pepper plant. It is valued for its antioxidant and antimicrobial properties.

BLACK SALT / KALA NAMAK: Black salt is a specialty salt used primarily in Pakistani and Indian cuisines. Unlike table salt, black salt is gray and has a sulfurous aroma. It adds a unique, savory, and slightly eggy flavor to dishes. Black salt is typically used to enhance chaats, chutneys, and various savory snacks. Himalayan pink salt can be substituted but will not quite replace the unique pungent flavor of black salt.

CARDAMOM / ELAICHI: Green cardamom and black cardamom differ in both flavor and appearance. Green cardamom pods are small and light green. They have a sweet, floral, and citrusy flavor, and they are often used in Pakistani desserts and beverages, as well as in savory dishes. Black cardamom pods are larger and dark brown. They have a smoky, earthy flavor and hints of camphor, and they are only used in savory dishes. For a milder flavor, substitute with nutmeg or cinnamon.

CAROM SEED / AJWAIN: Carom seeds are small seeds with a pungent, somewhat bitter flavor, similar to thyme and oregano. Commonly used in Pakistani cuisine, particularly in savory dishes, they impart a distinct aroma and also aid digestion.

CAYENNE RED PEPPER / LAAL MIRCH: Cayenne red pepper powder is the ever-present heat source in Pakistani food. It is used in both whole dried pepper form as well as in powder form, and it adds both heat and a vibrant red color to savory dishes. Note that cayenne red pepper powder is not the same as the chili powder or red chili powder in America. American chili powder is a spice blend, made with a mix of ground red chilies, cumin, paprika, garlic, salt, and onion powder. Cayenne red pepper powder is made from grinding only dried cayenne peppers. Milder substitutes for cayenne red chili powder include paprika and red pepper flakes.

CINNAMON / DALCHINI: Cinnamon is a versatile spice derived from the inner bark of trees of the genus *Cinnamomum*. It imparts a warm, sweet, and aromatic flavor with hints of spice and is widely used in both sweet and savory dishes in Pakistani cooking. Nutmeg or allspice can be used as substitutes.

CITRIC ACID POWDER / TATRI: A natural acid found in citrus fruits like lemons and limes, citric acid has a tart, sour flavor and is often used as a flavoring agent, a preservative, or to add tartness to dishes. You can substitute with lemon juice or vinegar, adjusting the quantity to get the level of sourness and acidity you desire.

CLOVES / LAUNG: Cloves, the aromatic flower buds harvested from the clove tree, give a warm, sweet, and earthy flavor to dishes. Widely used in both sweet and savory Pakistani dishes, cloves are also used to perk up drinks and in pickling.

CORIANDER / DHANIA SEEDS: Coriander seeds may be used as whole seeds, crushed seeds, i.e., hand crushed with a mortar and pestle, or in powder form with seeds ground fine in a spice grinder. Coriander seeds give a warm, citrusy, and slightly nutty flavor to savory dishes. Coriander or cilantro leaves are an herb and not to be confused with the seeds of the plant.

CUMIN / ZEERA: Along with coriander, cumin seeds are an essential spice in most Pakistani dishes. Like coriander seeds, cumin seeds can also be used whole, crushed, or powdered, depending on the recipe. They add earthy and warm tones to a dish.

DRIED MANGO POWDER / AMCHOOR: Dried mango powder is made from raw green mangoes that are dried and then ground to a fine powder. It infuses dishes with a tangy, sour, and fruity flavor, with a hint of sweetness. It is commonly used in Pakistani cuisine to brighten chutneys and marinades. Lemon or lime juice may be substituted but will lack the mango powder's unique fruity undertones. Tamarind paste can also provide a similar tanginess.

DRIED WHOLE RED CHILI PEPPERS: Sun-drying red chili peppers makes them shriveled and brittle in appearance, while intensifying their heat and aroma. They add spice and texture to many curries, stews, and rice dishes in Pakistani cuisine, and they are a common ingredient in the tarka or bhagar process (page 159), releasing their flavors and aroma when sautéed in hot oil. For recipes in this book that call for whole dried red peppers, dried Indian red chili peppers available in Indian/Pakistani stores and dried Mexican chilies like chile de arbol and pasilla chile available in most grocery stores all work well. Dried Sichuan chili peppers have a different and distinctive taste from Indian and Mexican red chilies and are *not* recommended for Pakistani dishes.

FENNEL SEED / SAUNF: Fennel seed, or saunf, is known for its distinctively licorice-like flavor. It's a staple in culinary creations worldwide, though it's used sparingly in Pakistani foods. Beyond its culinary uses, fennel seed is valued for its medicinal properties, known to aid digestion and alleviate coughs, and is often found in herbal remedies. Aniseed can be used as a substitute.

FENUGREEK SEEDS / METHI DANA: Fenugreek seeds have a nutty, somewhat acrid flavor, adding depth and aroma to dishes. Use them sparingly as fenugreek seeds can make your dish a bit bitter. Fenugreek seeds should not be confused with dried fenugreek leaves, which are a common dried herb used in Pakistani dishes.

GARLIC / LEHSUN: Aromatic and pungent, garlic is the workhorse spice of Pakistani cuisine, and, alongside onion and ginger, the fundamental ingredient in nearly all savory dishes. Garlic cloves are often minced, chopped, or pureed into garlic paste to release their flavor before being sautéed in ghee or oil. In our recipes, we primarily use garlic paste, not whole or minced garlic. Garlic paste can be bought in most stores or made at home by blitzing a cup of garlic cloves with a few tablespoons of water in a blender. If using whole cloves or minced garlic, ½ teaspoon of garlic paste equals 1 garlic clove or 1 teaspoon of minced garlic.

GINGER / ADRAK: Warm, spicy, and aromatic, ginger is a staple ingredient in Pakistani cuisine. Ginger is often sautéed with onions and garlic as a base for curries, stews, and stir-fries. It is also used as a finishing garnish in julienned or finely chopped form. Ginger is typically used in minced or pureed, i.e., paste form. Nearly all recipes in this book use ginger in paste form. If you do not have ginger paste on hand, you can substitute 1 teaspoon of finely chopped or minced ginger for ½ teaspoon of ginger paste.

KASHMIRI RED CHILI / KASHMIRI LAAL MIRCH: This is a vibrant red spice made from dried red chilies grown in Kashmir. It is most commonly used in powder form and has a mild to moderate heat profile compared with cayenne red chili powder. It imparts a rich, fruity, slightly earthy flavor and is used to add color and depth of flavor without overwhelming a dish with heat. A suitable substitute is paprika.

KASHMIRI TEA LEAVES / KASHMIRI CHAI KI PATTI: Kashmiri tea leaves are fragrant green tea leaves originating in Kashmir, used for making the famous Kashmir tea base called kahwa that gives Kashmiri tea its distinctive pink color. Several Kashmiri tea leaf brands are available in most South Asian stores.

MUSTARD SEEDS / SARSON: Mustard seeds are small seeds derived from the mustard plant. They have a sharp, pungent flavor and can be black, brown, or yellow in color, depending on the variety. Mustard seeds add depth and heat to dishes, as well as emulsify sauces. A suitable substitute is horseradish or wasabi powder for an equally pungent kick.

NIGELLA SEED / KALONGI: Nigella seeds are small black seeds with a bitter, peppery, slightly nutty flavor. They add depth and aroma to savory dishes—particularly vegetarian dishes—and pickles.

PANDAN FLOWER WATER / KEWRA WATER: Pandan flower water or simply pandan water is a fragrant floral water distilled from pandan flowers. It is used in Pakistani cuisine as an aroma and flavor agent. Its floral aroma is particularly desired in desserts and beverages, and rich specialties like biryanis and kormas.

PAPRI: Papri is a crispy snack made from refined flour maida or wheat flour atta, laced with spices like cumin and carom seeds, and deep-fried until golden brown and crunchy. Papri is a popular ingredient in chaats, a savory street food in Pakistani cuisine.

POMEGRANATE MOLASSES/CONCENTRATE: Pomegranate molasses is a thick, tangy, and sweet syrup made from reducing pomegranate juice. It has a rich, fruity flavor with a tart undertone and a sticky, syrup-like texture. Commonly used in Middle Eastern, North African, and South Asian cuisines, pomegranate molasses adds depth and complexity to dishes, sauces, marinades, and dressings.

POMEGRANATE SEEDS / ANAR DANA: Pomegranate seeds are the edible seeds found inside the pomegranate fruit. These reddish seeds have a sweet-and-tart flavor and a crunchy texture. They add a burst of color and crunchiness when used as a topping or ingredient in various dishes. Depending on the dish, we use seeds from a fresh pomegranate fruit chaat or dried seeds as seasoning for meats.

RAW PAPAYA / KUCCHA PAPITA: Raw papaya, the unripe fruit of the papaya tree, has a firm texture and a slightly sweet taste. Raw papaya can be used in chunks or in powder form. In Pakistani cooking, raw papaya powder is primarily used as a tenderizer for meats. Dried raw mango powder or store-bought meat tenderizer may be used as an alternative tenderizer. Regular fresh ripe papaya works just as well. No need to peel the papaya, but do discard seeds and grind well.

ROSE PRESERVE / GULKAND: Rose preserve, also known as *gulkand*, is a fragrant preserve made from rose petals and sugar. Rose preserve adds sweet, floral notes to ice cream, milkshakes, and other desserts and sweet beverages. Note that rose preserve is different from rose syrup or rose water.

ROSE SYRUP: Made with water, sugar, and rose petals or rose essence, rose syrup adds a floral and fragrant sweetness to Pakistani desserts and beverages. We always use Rooh Afza, the bestselling brand of Pakistani rose syrup available in Pakistani and Indian grocery stores in our desserts and sweet drinks, but any rose syrup will do.

ROSE WATER: Rose water is made by steeping rose petals in water, resulting in a fragrant liquid. Rose water adds a subtle floral aroma and flavor to dishes, without adding any sweetness. In Pakistani cuisine, it's commonly used in desserts and drinks, imparting a delicate rose flavor, but also in festive mains like biryani and rich meat curries, i.e, kormas.

SAFFRON / ZAFRAN: Saffron, derived from *Crocus sativus* flowers, graces Pakistani cuisine with its vibrant color, enticing aroma, and delicate taste, enriching dishes like biryani and a variety of desserts. Intensely aromatic and intensely expensive, it is used sparingly in various sweet and savory headlining dishes. Recognized for its antioxidants and mood enhancement benefits, saffron offers a unique culinary and wellness experience.

STAR ANISE / BADIAN KA PHOOL: Star anise has a distinct star shape and a slightly sweet, licorice-like flavor. Star anise is commonly used whole in specialties like biryani, or ground up as part of home-made garam masala powder. It is said to offer medicinal benefits, aiding digestion and promoting respiratory health. Aniseed or fennel seeds can be substituted.

TAMARIND / IMLI: Tamarind imparts a sweet-tangy flavor profile. It adds depth to curries, chutneys, and beverages across Pakistani cuisine. Besides its culinary uses, tamarind is well regarded for aiding digestion and promoting heart health. You can buy ready-to-use tamarind paste jars at any specialty store. Or you can get "compressed" seedless tamarind pulp slabs recommended in some of our recipes at any South Asian store, in many supermarkets, and, of course, on Amazon.

TURMERIC / HALDI: Turmeric, extracted from the *Curcuma longa* plant, has a vibrant golden color and warm, earthy flavor. It's a staple in cuisines worldwide, particularly in Pakistani curry dishes. Valued for its potent health benefits, including anti-inflammatory properties, turmeric adds depth and color to dishes.

Herbs

CILANTRO/CORIANDER LEAVES / DHANIA: Cilantro leaves are a popular herb in Pakistani cuisine, renowned for their fresh, citrusy flavor. It is an herb found in marinades, curries, salads, chutneys, and raitas. Its health benefits include aiding digestion and promoting heart health.

CURRY LEAVES / KARI PATTA: These aromatic leaves impart citrusy, herbal, and nutty flavors. They enhance curries, rice dishes, chutneys, and snacks alike. They are often quick-fried in hot oil for tempering, when they release their fragrant oils, infusing dishes with their distinct taste. Apart from culinary use, curry leaves are valued for aiding digestion and promoting hair health.

DRIED FENUGREEK LEAVES / KASOORI METHI: Dried fenugreek leaves are commonly used in Pakistani cuisine, particularly in dishes from the Punjab region. With a slightly bitter flavor and distinct aroma, they enhance curries, stews, and even flatbreads like naan. Fenugreek is also a source of fiber and antioxidants.

MINT / PUDINA: Mint is a versatile herb widely used in Pakistani cuisine. With its refreshing flavor and cooling properties, it enhances dishes such as chutneys and salads, and drinks like mint tea. Fresh pudina leaves lend a burst of freshness to both savory and sweet dishes. They're also valued for their potential health benefits, aiding digestion and soothing stomach discomfort.

Vegetables

EGGPLANTS: Though American eggplants are more widely available, we prefer the tender texture and sweeter taste of small, rounded Indian eggplants, Italian eggplants, or long, slender Japanese eggplants.

GREEN CHILIES / HARI MIRCH: Fresh green chili peppers add both heat and flavor to dishes, but they are not for everyone—which is why we very reluctantly make them optional in nearly all recipes. There are large differences in heat levels between Pakistani green chilies, hari mirch, and the chilies you will find in your local American grocery stores. Serrano peppers are fairly close in heat and taste;

jalapeños are, on average, milder; and Thai chilies are somewhat hotter. Unless otherwise specified, you may assume serrano chilies work for most of our recipes, feeling free to go milder jalapeño or hotter Thai chili. Deseed if you want to lower the heat level further.

ONIONS: Red, yellow, and white onions all work in this cookbook. We typically use organic yellow onions in our recipes.

POTATOES: Red, yellow, and russet brown potatoes all work in our recipes. Unless otherwise specified, we use russet potatoes.

SIZING: We sometimes refer to the vegetables needed in our recipes as "small" or "medium" or "large" in size especially staples such as onions, potatoes, and tomatoes. Note that a large onion typically yields 1½ to 2 cups of finely chopped onion, a medium onion about 1 cup, and a small onion ½ to ⅔ cup.

TOMATOES: Most of our recipes call for fresh ripe tomatoes. But canned peeled tomatoes also work. Some recipes explicitly call for tomato paste for its smoother texture and more concentrated color. Canned tomato sauce is to be avoided.

Rice, Flour, Noodles, and Lentils

ALL-PURPOSE FLOUR / MAIDA: Maida is a South Asian all-purpose flour, closely resembling cake flour or all-purpose white flour in the United States. A refined, fine-grained wheat flour with neutral taste, maida is used in making naans, puris, and parathas as well as desserts and pastries. While not as nutritious as whole wheat flour, all-purpose flour is your best bet for producing delicate, airy results in baking and soft and tender textures in bread making.

BASMATI RICE: Basmati rice, revered for its delicate fragrance and long, slender grains, is a staple in Pakistani cuisine. With its distinct aroma and fluffy texture, plain white basmati rice is the perfect accompaniment to various dishes. And all rice specialties, from biryanis to pulaos, must be made with high quality basmati rice. Basmati rice is known for its lower glycemic index, making it a healthier option compared to other rice varieties. Accept no substitutes.

CHICKPEA FLOUR / BESAN: Chickpea flour or gram flour, also known as besan, is a common ingredient in Pakistani cuisine. Made from ground chickpeas, it has a nutty flavor and fine texture. It is used in various savory and sweet dishes, and in batter as a thickening agent. It is gluten-free and higher in protein than wheat flour, making it a nutritious choice.

FALOODA NOODLES / FALOODA SEV: These thin, translucent noodles made from cornstarch or arrowroot are used in Pakistani desserts and specialty beverages. They have a gelatinous texture and readily absorb flavors, making them a popular ingredient in falooda, a refreshing dessert beverage. You will find them in nearly all Indian/Pakistani grocery stores.

LENTILS / DAAL: Rich in protein, fiber, and essential nutrients, lentils are a staple in everyday Pakistani meals. In Pakistani cooking, lentils can be whole with the husk or skin on or split husked and split in half. Whole lentils maintain their individual grains and take longer to cook. Split lentils tenderize and mush up leading to the lentil curry consistency that is usually desired. Most of our recipes use split lentils. We recommend soaking the lentils overnight, if possible. Soaking lentils in water for several hours breaks down the hard-to-digest protein called lectin, thus enhancing nutrient absorption. Here are a few of the most popular daals we use:

RED LENTILS / MASOOR DAAL: Red lentils, or masoor daal, are the quick-cooking staple lentil of the Pakistani kitchen. Both whole and split red lentils are used. Whole red lentils have a brown color and are used when making black lentils kaali masoor daal or kaali daal. Split red lentils husked and split in halves have a reddish-orange hue. They have a mild, earthy flavor and creamy texture when cooked.

SPLIT MUNG BEANS / MOONG DAAL: Split mung beans, also known as moong daal, are light yellow in color and cook quickly. They have a delicate, slightly sweet flavor and soft texture. Moong and masoor are the two most common daals is Pakistani cuisine.

SPLIT BENGAL GRAM OR BABY CHICKPEAS / CHANA DAAL: Split Bengal gram or baby chickpeas, also known as chana daal, is a pale-yellow lentil and has a nutty flavor with a slightly grainy texture. It takes longer to cook compared to masoor and moong daal but is worth the wait for its hearty taste. It is the most common lentil used in meat-and-lentil dishes.

WHOLE WHITE LENTILS / MAASH OR URAD DAAL: Whole white lentils, known as maash or urad daal, are creamy and nutty. Often slow-cooked with spices and tomatoes, they are the preferred lentil in haleem.

PARBOILED SELA BASMATI RICE: Sela basmati rice, also known as parboiled rice or simply sela rice, is a popular variant of basmati rice in Pakistani cuisine. It undergoes a unique parboiling process before milling, resulting in grains that are firmer and less sticky than regular white rice, making it a more forgiving rice choice for pulaos and biryanis, where it adds a nutty flavor and fluffy texture. It retains more nutrients compared to white rice, making it a healthier choice.

PEELED WHEAT / HALEEM WHEAT: Haleem wheat is a key ingredient in the beloved Pakistani dish haleem. Also known as broken wheat, peeled wheat, or cracked wheat, haleem wheat is essential to achieving the thick and creamy consistency characteristic of haleem. Cracked bulgur can be substituted.

ROASTED VERMICELLI / SEVIYAN: Roasted vermicelli is a thin wheat noodle, golden brown in color due to the roasting process it undergoes. The roasting enhances its flavor and gives it a nutty aroma. In Pakistani cooking, roasted vermicelli is most commonly used to make Eid desserts such as sheer khurma.

SEMOLINA / SOOJI: Semolina, or sooji, is a coarse durum wheat flour commonly used in Indian and Pakistani cuisines. With its gritty texture and nutty flavor, sooji is found in both sweet and savory dishes. It is a key ingredient in Pakistani desserts like sooji halwa.

WHOLE WHEAT FLOUR / ATTA: Whole wheat flour, or atta, holds a central place in Pakistani cuisine. Milled from whole wheat grains, atta has a nutty flavor and coarse texture. It serves as the foundation for various traditional dishes, including roti, chapati, and paratha. With its high fiber content and nutrients, atta is a wholesome choice. It's cherished for its role in Pakistani households, where it forms the basis of everyday meals.

Dairy

PANEER: Paneer cottage cheese or Indian cottage cheese is commonly used in vegetarian South Asian dishes as an alternative protein source to meat. Made by curdling milk with an acidic agent like lemon juice or vinegar, paneer is then pressed to form solid blocks. Its protein richness and its ability to absorb flavors makes it ideal for marinating and grilling. Its soft texture also lends itself well to stews and curries like paneer tikka and saag paneer. Firm tofu or halloumi can be used as substitutes.

YOGURT / DAHI: Made by fermenting milk with live cultures, yogurt, or dahi, is used in a wide array of Pakistani savory and sweet dishes. It is used as a base in curries, in meat marinades, and as a cooling accompaniment to spicy curries, biryanis, and kebabs. Dahi is also a key ingredient of traditional Pakistani drinks like lassi. In most cases, be sure to whip the yogurt until smooth before adding it to a curry sauce or when using it in dips and raitas. Unless otherwise specified, e.g., the Greek yogurt we suggest for our eggplant dip, we recommend using plain, regular yogurt, and whole milk is preferred to low-fat or fat-free versions.

EQUIPMENT AND UTENSILS

GRINDER: If you don't have a spice grinder or coffee grinder, buy ground spices and grind the ones that don't come ground e.g., anise seed with a mortar and pestle. If you use a grinder for spices, it's best to have a dedicated grinder that you don't also use for coffee.

HANDI: A deep cooking vessel with a wide bottom, used for slow-cooking curries. Substitute: Dutch oven or a heavy-bottomed pot.

KARAHI: Similar to a wok, the karahi is a deep, circular cooking pot with handles, used for deep-frying and making curries. Substitute: deep skillet or a wok.

MORTAR AND PESTLE: Made of strong materials like marble and occasionally wood, the mortar and pestle are used to crush and grind whole spices, releasing their essential oils.

PRESSURE COOKER: Great for cooking lentils, beans, and tough meats quickly, pressure cookers are widely used in Pakistani and Indian households. Instant Pot works just as well.

TAWA: A flat, round griddle used for making rotis and parathas. Substitute: flat griddle or a cast-iron skillet

TECHNIQUES

Bhunna or Bhunnai
Sautéing Ingredients in Oil

Bhunna is a cooking technique in Pakistani cuisine that involves sautéing and roasting ingredients in oil on medium-low heat to enhance their flavors. Commonly used for onions, garlic, masala pastes, tomatoes, and meats, bhunna allows spices to release their flavors into the oil and adds depth and richness to dishes. You begin with heating oil or ghee, followed by the addition of onion, then ginger and garlic if called for, then spices e.g., turmeric, cumin, and coriander, and then other ingredients e.g., tomatoes or meats. A little water may be added in the process to aid in cooking the ingredients and preventing them from sticking to the pot. As the spices and other ingredients cook, they release their natural oils and sugars, resulting in intensified flavors and aromas.

In some dishes you have to repeat the bhunna process more than once. For instance, bhunnai may be done to first make the perfect onion-spices-tomato base, and then repeated after the meat is added to and cooked in the tomato base.

The bhunna process is successfully finished when the oil in which the ingredients are cooked separates and rises to the top, and you see a nice shimmer over the ingredients.

Dum
Steaming

Dum, a traditional cooking method in Pakistani cuisine, involves slow-cooking food in a sealed vessel over low heat. This technique allows the ingredients to cook gently in their own juices, resulting in tender and flavorful dishes. Commonly used for biryanis, curries, and kebabs, dum cooking infuses the food with rich, aromatic flavors. The sealed vessel traps moisture, ensuring that the dish remains moist and succulent. Dum cooking requires patience and attention to detail but rewards with dishes that are bursting with complex flavors and irresistible aromas, making it a cherished culinary tradition in Pakistani households.

Tarka or Bhagar
Tempering Spices in Oil

Tarka, an essential cooking technique in Pakistani cuisine, involves adding seasoned oil or ghee to dishes to enhance flavor. Typically done at the end of cooking, tarka infuses the dish with aromatic spices and herbs. Common ingredients for tarka include cumin seeds, mustard seeds, curry leaves, and dried red chilies, among others. The heated oil or ghee releases the flavors of the spices, elevating the taste of the dish. Tarka adds depth and complexity to various Pakistani dishes, including daals, curries, and rice.

I.

HALKA-PULKA

✦•❖•❖•❖•❖•❖•❖•❖•❖•❖•❖•✦

Snacks and Starters

ON ONION PAKORA

✦✦✦✦✦✦✦✦✦✦✦✦✦✦✦✦✦✦✦✦✦✦✦✦✦✦✦✦✦✦

This was the snack of all our lazy, rainy yesterdays. Monsoons in Pakistan seemed to summon chai and pakoras. Through half-shuttered windows would enter the pleasant din of rain and cool exhalations of moist earth. Before us would appear steaming cups of chai and platters of onion pakoras, swooped just moments before from hot oil, their tanned ridges titillating us with promises of spicy crunch.

Only a few minutes ago, slivered onions had been mixed into an unctuous batter of gram flour, baking soda, and spices. Dollops of this mixture had been hand-scooped and glided into hot oil. Batch after batch of newly minted pakoras had been strained out with a mesh skimmer and tossed onto paper-lined platters for us.

We would swipe a pakora on mint-coriander chutney and ketchup, catching green and red flecks on its spiky skin; devour a generous bite of crisp shell, pliant onion, and light sponge; then chase it down with sweet, hot tea.

These versatile onion fritters and their potato, spinach, pepper, and eggplant cousins were also the opening salvo of all our Ramadan iftars, the breaking of the daily fast at sunset. The accompanying drink then would be chilled rose-syrup-flavored water or milk.

No matter the occasion, no one ever truthfully claimed to eat only one pakora in a sitting. Anyone who claimed to eat only two also lied.

ONION PAKORA Ⓥ

Onion Fritter

½ cup chickpea flour
   (besan)
1 tablespoon cornstarch
1 teaspoon salt
½ teaspoon cumin seeds
1 teaspoon coriander seeds
¼ teaspoon carom seeds
   (ajwain)
½ teaspoon red chili flakes
¼ teaspoon ground turmeric
1 large onion, thinly sliced
1 small potato, julienned
1 jalapeño, julienned
Oil, for deep-frying
Hari Chutney (page 205),
   for serving
Imli Chutney (page 206),
   for serving
Ketchup, for serving

A teatime snack, a mealtime appetizer, a quick fix for unexpected guests, and an end-of-fast special during Ramadan, the onion pakora's versatility comes from the fact that it is nearly as easy to make as it is to devour. Our recipe sneaks in some julienned potatoes to add another layer of texture.

▾▾▾▾▾▾▾▾▾▾▾▾▾▾▾▾▾▾▾▾▾▾▾▾▾▾▾▾

PRO TIPS

Heat oil in a karahi, a Dutch oven, or a deep pot or saucepan. Don't use a shallow frying pan.

The frying oil should remain medium hot about 350 degrees F: too hot, and the fritters will turn dark brown without being cooked through; too cold, and the fritters will absorb oil and become soggy and greasy.

We recommend you fry one fritter first to taste and adjust seasoning before frying the rest.

* In a mixing bowl, combine the flour (sifted beforehand), cornstarch, salt, cumin, coriander, carom seeds, cayenne, and turmeric. Add the onion, potato, jalapeño, and 2 tablespoons of water. Mix well. The mixture should be on the dryer side, just clumping together. Set aside for 20 minutes to let vegetables sweat further.

* In a karahi, wok, or deep pot, heat 2 inches of oil over medium heat until the oil reaches 350 degrees F. Test that the oil is ready for frying by dropping ½ teaspoon of batter into the oil and checking that it sizzles and bubbles to the top.

* Give the batter one last mix before frying. Using a tablespoon or your hand, if you are an expert, gently glide dollops, i.e., rounded tablespoons, of the onion-batter mix into the hot oil.

* Deep-fry for about 2 minutes before flipping the fritters over and frying for another 2 to 3 minutes, until golden brown.

* Scoop out the fritters with a slotted spoon and drain on a paper towel to absorb any excess oil.

* Serve hot with hari chutney, imli chutney, and ketchup.

ALOO PAKORA ⓥᵍ
Potato Fritter

¾ cup chickpea flour
  (besan)
1 tablespoon cornstarch
1 teaspoon salt (or to taste)
¾ teaspoon cayenne red
  chili powder (or to taste)
½ teaspoon cumin seeds
¼ teaspoon carom seeds
  (ajwain)
1 large russet potato or small
  red potatoes
Oil, for deep-frying
Hari Chutney (page 205), for
  serving
Ketchup, for serving

PRO TIPS

Heat oil in a karahi, a
Dutch oven, or a deep pot
or saucepan. Don't use a
shallow frying pan.

The frying oil should remain
medium hot about 350
degrees F: too hot, and the
fritters will turn dark brown
without being cooked
through; too cold, and the
fritters will absorb oil and
become soggy and greasy.

We recommend you fry
one fritter first to taste and
adjust seasoning before
frying the rest.

This recipe uses a thinner batter than the Onion Pakora and
is extremely versatile. Instead of potatoes, you can also use
other vegetables like sliced eggplants, spinach leaves, or cauli-
flower florets.

▼▼▼▼▼▼▼▼▼▼▼▼▼▼▼▼▼▼▼▼▼▼▼▼▼

• In a mixing bowl, combine the flour (sifted beforehand), cornstarch, salt, cayenne, cumin, and carom seeds. Add ⅓ cup of
  water and mix, adding more water as needed to get a pancake
  batter consistency. Set aside for 5 to 10 minutes.

• Peel the potato and slice into rounds about ⅛ inch thick using a
  mandoline or knife. Soak the sliced potatoes in water until ready
  to use.

• In a karahi, wok, or deep pot, heat 2 inches of oil over medium
  heat until the oil reaches 350 degrees F. Test that the oil is ready
  for frying by dropping ½ teaspoon of batter into the oil and
  checking that it sizzles and bubbles to the top.

• Dip the potato slices in the batter, a few at a time, and then glide
  each battered potato into the hot oil.

• Deep-fry for 2 to 3 minutes before flipping over. Fry for another
  2 minutes or so on the other side, until golden brown on both sides.

• Scoop out the fritters with a slotted spoon and place on a paper
  towel to absorb excess oil.

• Serve with hari chutney and ketchup.

> **VARIATIONS**
>
> **SPINACH PAKORA:** Replace the potato with one bunch of mature spin-
> ach leaves (not baby spinach).
>
> **KALE PAKORA:** Replace the potato with kale leaves.
>
> **EGGPLANT PAKORA:** Replace the potato with 2 eggplants sliced
> ⅛ to ¼ inch thick.

ON MEMONI SAMOSA

❖·❖

To those of us who grew up on this snack, the samosa belongs among the great triangular concepts of human civilization, right alongside the Pythagorean theorem and the love triangle.

The Memoni variant of this labor of love starts with minced meat, spices, green chilies, and herbs slow-cooked for hours. A mound of this filling is wrapped in a delicate dough sari, fried to crackling perfection, and, finally, its bronzed skin is rouged with a sprinkle of chaat masala.

We who first met this snack as toddlers know that a samosa must be savored hot. With our first crunch escape wisps of aromatic steam, and we smell once again our childhood.

May we always savor all three sides of a great samosa: taste, texture, and nostalgia.

MEMONI SAMOSA
Savory Green Masala Chicken Turnovers

1 bunch (about 6) green
   onions, very finely
   chopped

For the green masala paste:
1 cup chopped cilantro
½ cup mint
3-4 green chilies, deseed to
   reduce spice level
6 garlic cloves
1 tablespoon cumin seeds
1 (1-inch) piece ginger

For the meat filling:
1 pound ground chicken
1 tablespoon Garam Masala
1½ teaspoons salt
2 tablespoons freshly
   squeezed lemon juice

*For forming and frying
   samosas:*
2 tablespoons all-purpose
   flour
1 packet of egg roll wrappers
Oil, for deep-frying
1 teaspoon Chaat Masala
   (page 214)
Hari Chutney (page 205),
   for serving
Imli Chutney (page 206),
   for serving

This is the appetizer that helped get Zareen's into the *Michelin Guide*! The secret to our Memoni samosa is the green masala paste used to season the ground meat. We use ground chicken at Zareen's but lamb and beef work just as well.

▾▾▾▾▾▾▾▾▾▾▾▾▾▾▾▾▾▾▾▾▾▾▾▾▾▾▾

PREPARING THE FILLING:

◆ Remove any excess water from the onion with paper towels.
   Set aside.

MAKE THE GREEN MASALA PASTE:

◆ In a blender or food processor, blend all of the ingredients with
   ½ cup of water to make a smooth paste. Set aside.

◆ In a bowl, mix the ground chicken with the green masala paste,
   garam masala, and salt.

◆ In a Dutch oven, cook the chicken mixture over medium
   heat until all the water evaporates, stirring occasionally and
   breaking apart any lumps, 20 to 30 minutes. The meat should be
   completely dry so the samosas can come out crisp.

◆ Add in the lemon juice and mix well.

◆ Turn off the heat, take the chicken mixture out, and place it on a
   wide platter to cool and allow any excess water to evaporate.

◆ When the chicken mixture is cool, add the onion and mix well.
   Taste the mixture and adjust seasoning if needed.

FORMING THE SAMOSAS:

◆ In a small bowl, make a thin paste with the flour and ⅓ cup
   of water.

◆ Cut the egg roll wrappers into 3 long rectangular strips about
   2.5 inches wide and 5 to 6 inches long.

◆ Visualize each strip as a top square and a bottom rectangle. Place
   a tablespoon of the meat filling in the middle of the top square.

◆ Fold one edge of the top square.

◆ Fold again to close the filling and make a triangle out of the
   top square.

◆ Fold the triangle onto the bottom rectangle.

- You will have a small part of the strip left. Bring that over and seal using a little flour paste.
- Use as many wrappers as needed to use up the filling. The left-over wrappers can be stored in the fridge.

FRYING THE SAMOSAS:

- Heat 2 inches of oil in a karahi, wok, or deep pan over medium heat until the oil reaches 350 degrees F.
- Fry the samosas for 1 to 2 minutes on one side before flipping over. Fry for another 1 to 2 minutes on the other side, until golden brown on both sides. Do not over brown the samosas.
- Scoop out with a slotted spoon and place on a paper towel to absorb excess oil. Sprinkle with chaat masala.
- Serve hot with hari chutney and imli chutney on the side.

DAHI BARAY ⓥ

Chickpea Dumplings in Yogurt with Chutneys

For the dumplings:
1 cup yellow lentil (moong)
    or white lentil (urad)
1 tablespoon cumin seeds
1 (1-inch) piece ginger,
    coarsely chopped
2 green chilies, deseeded to
    reduce heat
1 teaspoon salt
¼ teaspoon baking powder
Oil, for deep-frying

For the yogurt:
2 cups yogurt
¾ teaspoon salt (or to taste)
4 tablespoons sugar
    (or to taste)
1 tablespoon Chaat Masala
    (page 215)
2 tablespoons Imli Chutney
    (page 206) optional
2 tablespoons Hari Chutney
    (page 205) optional

PRO TIP

After you have taken the
dumplings out of the water
bath, you can refrigerate or
freeze them for later use.

One of the most popular street foods in Pakistan, dahi baray
or dahi balay are lightly spiced lentil dumplings topped with
tangy yogurt and sweet and spicy chutneys. A staple of the
iftar breaking of fast meal in Ramadan, dahi baray work just
as well as a standalone snack as they do as an appetizer where
they often overshadow the main course.

▾▾▾▾▾▾▾▾▾▾▾▾▾▾▾▾▾▾▾▾▾▾▾▾▾▾▾

MAKE THE DUMPLINGS:

⬥ In a medium bowl, soak the lentils in enough water to cover.
  Leave overnight or for at least 2 hours. Drain when ready to use.

⬥ In a blender, add the lentils, cumin seeds, ginger, green chilies, and
  about ½ cup to ¾ cup of water. Blend until you get a smooth paste.

⬥ Pour the batter into a mixing bowl. Add the salt and baking powder. Mix thoroughly with an electric mixer or hand whisk. This
  helps incorporate air into the batter, making it light and smooth in
  texture. Set aside.

⬥ In a deep pan, heat at least 2 to 3 inches of oil to 325 degrees F
  over medium heat.

⬥ Using a teaspoon, drop one spoonful of batter into the oil at
  a time. Fry dumplings while turning until golden brown, 8 to
  12 minutes. If batter starts to stick to the spoon, use the back
  of another spoon to gently glide out the batter.

⬥ Scoop out with a slotted spoon and place on a paper towel to
  absorb excess oil.

⬥ Prepare a water bath by filling a shallow bowl with room
  temperature water.

⬥ Soak the dumplings in the water bath for 15 minutes.

⬥ Drain the water and lightly squeeze the dumplings with your
  hands to remove excess water.

MAKE THE YOGURT:

⬥ In a separate bowl, whisk the yogurt with the salt, sugar, and
  ¾ cup of water until smooth. Taste and adjust salt and sugar as
  needed.

⬥ Put the dumplings in a serving dish. Pour the seasoned yogurt
  over the dumplings. Sprinkle with chaat masala. Drizzle chutneys
  to serve.

CHOLAY CHAAT ⓥ
Tangy Chickpea Salad

For the chickpeas:
2 (15-ounce) cans chickpeas, about 3 cups, drained
½ teaspoon baking soda
1 teaspoon salt (or to taste)
¼ teaspoon cayenne red chili powder (optional)

For the yogurt:
1 cup plain yogurt
¼ cup sugar
1 teaspoon salt

1 medium potato (to yield about 1 cup cubed potato)
2 tablespoons finely chopped red onion
1 finely chopped tomato
½ cup finely chopped fresh cilantro
3 finely chopped fresh green chilies (optional)
2 tablespoons Hari Chutney (page 205)
2 tablespoons Imli Chutney (page 206)
1 teaspoon Chaat Masala (page 214)
1 (200-gram) packet of Papri/ Papdi (savory crackers available in South Asian grocery stores) crushed

PRO TIP

Chaats are all about experimentation: feel free to vary the amount of onions, tomatoes, green chilies, cilantro, tamarind chutney, and chaat masala per serving.

Our recipe is based on the offerings of the street vendors in the Saddar neighborhood of Karachi: chickpeas cholay topped with fresh garden vegetables and herbs, yogurt, tamarind chutney, and chaat masala. It's best served with a dollop of lightly sweetened yogurt or when paired with Dahi Baray (page 61). A perfect any-time-of-day snack? Or a side at lunch or dinner? Or the entirety of a light meal? Yes.

▾▾▾▾▾▾▾▾▾▾▾▾▾▾▾▾▾▾▾▾▾▾▾▾▾▾▾▾▾

- In a medium saucepan, add the chickpeas, 1 cup of water, and the baking soda, and heat over medium heat for about 10 minutes, to soften the chickpeas.

- When the chickpeas become tender, mash a few chickpeas with a spoon, leaving the rest intact. Add the salt and cayenne and mix, adjusting with more salt as needed. Set aside.

- Boil the potato skin on in a medium saucepan until tender but not mushy. Allow to cool, then peel away skin with fingers and chop into ½-inch cubes.

MAKE THE YOGURT:

- In a bowl, whisk the yogurt with sugar and salt, adjusting salt to taste.

TO SERVE FAMILY STYLE:

- Pour the chickpeas into a shallow casserole dish. Spread the sweetened yogurt over the chickpeas.

- Add a layer of potato cubes, followed by onion, tomato, cilantro, and green chilies.

- Drizzle with hari chutney and imli chutney, and sprinkle generously with chaat masala. Top with a sprinkling of crushed Papri.

FOR AN INDIVIDUAL SERVING:

- Place one-fourth of the chickpeas in an individual bowl.

- Add one-fourth of the sweetened yogurt.

- Top with one-fourth each of the potato, onion, tomato, cilantro, and green chilies.

- Top with hari chutney, imli chutney, a generous sprinkling of chaat masala, and crushed Papri.

FRUIT CHAAT ⓥ

Sweet and Tangy Fruit Salad

1½ cups sliced banana

1 cup diced, deseeded
orange (1 small orange)

1 cup diced apple
(1 large apple)

½ cup diced mango
(if unavailable, substitute
with pear)

½ cup grapes, cut in halves

½ cup diced guava
(optional)

½ cup orange juice, preferably freshly squeezed

2 tablespoons fresh pome-
granate seeds (optional)

2 tablespoons sugar
(or to taste)

1 teaspoon freshly ground
black pepper

1 teaspoon Chaat Masala
(page 214)

In Pakistan, the most commonly used fruits for this tangy
salad are bananas, apples, guavas, pears, and grapes. You
should feel free to use in-season fruits available near you. This
is a refreshing standalone snack, a welcome item at high tea,
or a luncheon appetizer or side.

▾▾▾▾▾▾▾▾▾▾▾▾▾▾▾▾▾▾▾▾▾▾▾▾▾▾▾

- Place all the fruit in a large bowl.

- Add in the orange juice, pomegranate seeds, sugar, pepper, and
  chaat masala. Use a fork to mix well. Taste, and adjust with more
  sugar or chaat masala as needed.

- Let the fruit salad sit in the fridge for at least 30 minutes.

- Give it a final mix before serving. Leftover fruit chaat can be
  refrigerated and keeps well for a day or two but not much more.

NADIYA HUSSAIN
Chef and Author

CHOSEN CHARITY: WATERAID

We asked Nadiya to select the charity she would like us to support. She selected WaterAid: "I have worked with WaterAid for eight years now. They are a UK charity that works tirelessly to provide clean, safe water to people around the world. They work closely with communities in Bangladesh, which made the appeal to work with them even stronger."

NADIYA'S MESSAGE: FROM SURVIVING TO THRIVING

"I was raised in an environment where it was always 'survival.' Everyone was simply surviving, from wage to wage, from day to day, month to month. They didn't really have a choice, they were immigrants and they had responsibilities that surpassed that of their own nuclear family. They had responsibilities that meant helping everyone. It has been a habit that I have picked up and in doing so for a long time I realized that I didn't know how to thrive: I was simply always surviving. It is important to survive, but if you can, step back and ask yourself: Are you thriving? If you are not, how can you?"

WHY WE LOVE NADIYA

Her victory speech on winning the 2015 *Great British Bake Off* moved the show's judges, all of us fans, and, we suspect, most of South Asia to tears of pride. Since then, British Bangladeshi Nadiya Hussain has authored over sixteen books ranging from cookery to fiction, hosted and headlined several TV shows, launched her own home-ware collection, received numerous awards and recognitions including an MBE, a British Order of Chivalry, and baked the ninetieth birthday cake for Queen Elizabeth II. She has lived up to her memorable speech in 2015: "I'm never gonna put boundaries on myself ever again. I'm never gonna say I can't do it. I'm never gonna say 'maybe.' I'm never gonna say, 'I don't think I can.' I can and I will." More importantly, she has inspired millions of girls and women to also live up to her words.

A FAVORITE EAT: CHICKEN KORMA

So what is this celebrated foodie's favorite dish? "Chicken korma. Not the kind you get at the local Indian restaurant. The kind that we ate as small children–simple, wholesome, and aromatic, not tampered with or changed to something inauthentic. Chicken korma is one of the most memorable dishes we ate growing up and I still make it for my own children today."

DESI PALEO SALAD

For the yogurt-ranch dressing:

½ cup ranch dressing

2 tablespoons plain yogurt

For the salad:

5 ounces spring mix salad greens

½ cup peeled and deseeded orange slices

1 Persian cucumber, sliced

1 medium tomato, sliced

Few slivers of sweet onion (optional)

¼ cup cranberries or raisins

½ recipe Grilled Chicken Boti (page 99) approximately 2 chicken breasts

¼ cup Imli Chutney (page 206)

¼ cup sunflower seeds

This is the signature salad at Zareen's: a marriage made in paleo heaven between our popular Orange Is the New Green Salad and our bestselling Grilled Chicken Boti. Going low carb never tasted this good. To go full paleo, eliminate or reduce the amount of cranberries to lower the sugar content.

To mix it up, try swapping the Grilled Chicken Boti with Chapli Kabab (page 129), Fish Shami Kababs (page 140), or Aloo Tikki (page 151). Or skip the meat entirely to enjoy the vegetarian Orange Is the New Green Salad in all its light and bright goodness.

▾▾▾▾▾▾▾▾▾▾▾▾▾▾▾▾▾▾▾▾▾▾▾▾▾▾▾

MAKE THE YOGURT-RANCH DRESSING:

- In a small bowl, mix the ranch dressing and yogurt using a fork.

MAKE THE SALAD:

- In a large bowl, toss the spring mix with the orange slices, cucumber, tomato, onions (optional), and cranberries.

- Chop the grilled chicken boti into bite-size chunks.

- Top the salad with the grilled chicken (use about ¾ cup of cooked chicken per serving). Drizzle with the yogurt-ranch dressing, and cross drizzle with imli chutney. Sprinkle with sunflower seeds and serve.

ON BUN KABABS

If Burns Road is the ultimate food street (and it is), then bun kababs (Pakistani sliders) are its ultimate street food.

Up the road from arguably the world's best haleem, nihari, gola kabab, and kheer hotspots, and across the road from the famous Fresco Sweets serving dahi baray to die for, stands a small tehla stall that is mobbed daily by bun kabab addicts. The bun kabab tehla has no name, only a sign saying "humari koi aur branch nahin," "we don't have any other branch." Back in the sixties and seventies, it stood right opposite Azad Tailor Shop. So it became known as "Azad kay Bun Kabab." Azad Tailor was replaced by an optical store, but families in the area continued calling it Azad's Bun Kabab. It still has no official name.

If you are ever fortunate enough to make it to "Azaad's," you will realize just how much anticipation is the better part of gastronomy. Join your comrade bun kabab addicts to watch the kabab patty being dipped into vigorously whipped eggs and placed on the open tawa griddle where the sizzling kabab gains a floral fringe of omelet. Control yourself a few moments longer as the bun is grilled to a caramelized crispiness. Just a few seconds more as their special chutney is drizzled, with the effortless grace of thirty years of practice, onto willowy onion strands atop steaming kabab. Grab your paper-wrapped order and take your first bite, then marvel at how such culinary high art can come from such an anonymous little stall. But, after all, what's in a name?

SANA AMANAT
Maker of Superheroes

WHY WE LOVE SANA

The Pakistani American superheroine behind Marvel's first Muslim American superhero, Sana Amanat is the co-creator of Ms. Marvel (Kamala Khan). Ms. Marvel has sold over half a million paperbacks and has been adapted to a live-action series on Disney+ which Sana executive-produced. Sana also co-created the Women of Marvel podcast and panels at Comic-Con. Currently an executive of production and development at Marvel Studios, Sana has been at Marvel for 15 years creating content across the company's many platforms. Sana's superpower, it seems, is developing relatable and representative characters in the world of superheroes. And our world is so much the better for it.

CHOSEN CHARITY: PALESTINIAN CHILDREN'S RELIEF FUND (PCRF)

Founded in 1991 by concerned humanitarians in the United States, PCRF provides free medical care to thousands of injured and ill children yearly who lack local access to care. Over the years, PCRF has sent more than 2,000 affected children abroad for free medical care and sent thousands of doctors and nurses to provide tens of thousands of children free medical care in local hospitals. PCRF envisions a world where all children in the Middle East have access to quality medical care, humanitarian aid, and specialized surgical procedures.

SANA'S MESSAGE: ANYONE CAN BE A HERO

I am so fortunate to have had strong, powerful women in my life, starting with my mother and my grandmother. I made a South Asian, Muslim American girl from New Jersey a superhero to help remind women, especially Muslim women, they have great powers within themselves. When they see Kamala Khan, I hope that women feel proud, feel empowered, and feel seen. Above all, I hope they see that anyone, regardless of their looks or their "origin story," can be a hero.

A FAVORITE EAT: CHOLAY AND ALOO MUTTAR

While not a vegetarian, Sana's best-loved homecooked dishes are two of the most popular Pakistani vegetarian specialties: Cholay (Chickpea Stew) and Aloo Muttar (Potatoes and Green Peas).

To enjoy a delicious chickpea stew at your home, follow our Lahori Cholay recipe (page 162), accompanying the stew (as Sana would) with piping hot puris (page 197). For Aloo Muttar, follow our Zeera Aloo recipe (page 154) with the following additions: after the potatoes have been stir fried with the spices, add ⅓ cup frozen peas alongside the ½ cup of water required in the recipe, sprinkling a generous pinch of salt to season the peas. Cook until potatoes are done. Serve with fresh rotis.

BUN KABAB

Spicy Sliders with Egg-Dipped Ground-Chana-and-Chicken Patty

For the patties:

1 cup split Bengal gram
   (chana daal)
1 cup ground chicken
1 teaspoon Garam Masala
   (page 215) or store-bought
4 to 5 dried red chilies
1 (1-inch) piece ginger
5 to 6 garlic cloves
1 small onion, peeled and
   quartered
1½ teaspoons salt (or
   to taste)

2 eggs
Oil, for frying
8 to 10 slider buns, e.g.,
   King's Hawaiian Sweet
   Rolls or "Pav" buns available in Indian/Pakistani
   grocery stores
½ cup thinly sliced onions
10 to 12 teaspoons of
   Wicked Spicy Chutney
   (page 207) or a milder
   green chutney

Here we attempt to faithfully reproduce the famous bun kababs at Azaad's Bun Kabab stall on Burns Road in Karachi. However, you can easily vary the meat for the patties; ground chicken, lamb, and beef work equally well. The patties (kababs) themselves make great standalone snacks or robust toppings to a garden salad. If not using them to make bun kababs, you can choose to skip dipping them in the egg mixture before frying.

Any type of bun kababs is best accompanied by Masala Fries (page 75) and a cooling lassi (page 218).

▼▼▼▼▼▼▼▼▼▼▼▼▼▼▼▼▼▼▼▼▼▼▼▼▼▼

MAKE THE PATTIES:

- Cook the lentils in a Dutch oven with 2 cups of water, the chicken, garam masala, chilies, ginger, garlic, and onion, until the daal is fully cooked, that is, there are no hard centers in the lentils and the water is evaporated, leaving a fairly dry meat and lentil mixture, about 30 to 40 minutes. Add the salt toward the end, after the daal is cooked, adjusting salt to taste.

- Grind the mixture in a food processor while still hot. Set aside to cool.

- Shape into eight to ten ½-inch-thick patties, each about 3 inches in diameter.

- In a small bowl, separate the yolks from the egg whites and set the yolks aside. In a medium bowl, beat the egg whites until frothy. Lightly beat the yolks. Gently fold the lightly beaten yolks into the egg whites. Set aside.

- Heat 2 tablespoons of oil in a large frying pan or skillet.

- Dip each lentil-meat patty in the beaten eggs and shallow-fry for 2 to 3 minutes on each side until golden brown.

- Toast the buns face down on the skillet with a little oil or butter until crispy brown, about a minute or so. Turn over and lightly toast the top for about 30 seconds.

- Place each fried patty in a bun, and top with sliced onions and about a teaspoon or more of wicked spicy chutney. Serve immediately.

BOTI PARATHA ROLLS

1 recipe Grilled Chicken
Boti (page 99)
4 Lachha Paratha (page 189),
regular Paratha (page 184),
or ready-to-fry store-
bought parathas, cooked
1 medium onion, thinly sliced
2 tablespoons finely
chopped fresh mint
4 teaspoons Wicked Spicy
Chutney (page 207)
Hari Chutney (page 205) or
your favorite green chut-
ney, for drizzling (optional)
Sliced green chilies
(optional)

PRO TIP

In a rush? Buy ready-to-fry
parathas from your nearest
Indian/Pakistani grocery
store and focus on making
the filling at home!

Seaside picnics at Hawkes Bay, food fests after gully cricket, midnights out with schoolmates: all our memories of care-free youth seem to feature paratha rolls. All the indulgence of kababs and parathas in a travel-size package, paratha rolls are the portable snack of choice for Karachiwalas.

Our paratha roll recipe is a composite recipe that simply requires assembly once you have created or purchased the components: parathas, meat or vegetarian filling, chutneys, and onions. The paratha roll lends itself to variations; here we offer you Chicken Boti Paratha Rolls, Beef Gola Paratha Rolls, Aloo Tikki Paratha Rolls, and Zeera Aloo Paratha Rolls in an effort to recreate the legendary rolls at Silver Spoon Snacks off Tariq Road in Karachi. Paratha rolls go well with a side of Masala Fries (page 75), Karachi-Style Coleslaw (page 209), or a side salad.

▼▼▼▼▼▼▼▼▼▼▼▼▼▼▼▼▼▼▼▼▼▼▼▼

- Chop the grilled chicken boti into bite-size pieces.

- Place a 4-to-5-ounce portion of grilled chicken along the center of each paratha.

- Top the chicken with a few onion slices and about ½ tablespoon of mint.

- Drizzle 1 teaspoon of wicked spicy chutney or more to taste and some hari green chutney.

- Fold one side of the paratha to cover the filling and then fold the other side of the paratha over it to double enclose the filling. Unlike a burrito, both ends of the roll should remain open.

- Wrap the paratha roll in wax paper or aluminum foil to keep hot. Serve immediately.

VARIATIONS

BEEF GOLA PARATHA ROLLS: Substitute 4 Gola Kababs (page 126) for the grilled chicken boti. During assembly, place a kabab in each paratha and smash by hand to spread along the center of the paratha.

ALOO TIKKI PARATHA ROLLS: Substitute 8 Aloo Tikkis (page 151) for the grilled chicken boti use 2 aloo tikkis per roll. During assembly, shape and spread 2 tikkis evenly along the center of the paratha.

ZEERA ALOO PARATHA ROLLS: Substitute a full recipe of Zeera Aloo cumin-laced potatoes (page 154), divided into 4 servings, for the grilled chicken boti.

BAKED MASALA POTATO WEDGES

1½ pounds potatoes (about 2 large russet potatoes)

½ teaspoon salt

1 teaspoon red pepper flakes

½ teaspoon raw mango powder

½ teaspoon cumin seeds

Pinch of carom seeds (ajwain), optional or to taste

3 to 4 tablespoons olive oil or avocado oil, plus more for greasing

3 to 4 tablespoons rice flour or cornstarch

Garlic-Chili Ketchup (page 207), for serving

Hari Chutney (page 205), for serving

PRO TIP

Dried mango powder can be replaced with 1 tablespoon of freshly squeezed lemon juice.

Thick potato wedges are drizzled with olive oil, sprinkled with spices, and baked until crispy on the outside and tender inside. Never happier than when teamed up with your favorite kababs, burgers, or sliders. These also work well as a robust side to go with your morning eggs.

▼▼▼▼▼▼▼▼▼▼▼▼▼▼▼▼▼▼▼▼▼▼▼▼▼▼▼▼▼

• Preheat the oven to 400 degrees F. Grease a nonstick baking sheet.

• Peel the potatoes and cut them into ½-inch-thick wedges.

• In a medium bowl, toss the potatoes with the salt, red pepper flakes, mango powder, seeds, and oil with tongs until the wedges are well coated.

• Sprinkle the rice flour on the wedges and toss lightly.

• Spread the potato wedges on the prepared baking sheet and bake until crispy and golden brown, about 30 minutes.

• Serve hot with garlic-chili ketchup and hari chutney.

MASALA FRIES Ⓥ

Oil, for deep-frying
4 servings of frozen precut
  french fries (about 12 fries
  per serving)
1 to 2 teaspoons Chaat
  Masala (page 214) or use
  store-bought
Red Hot Garlic-Chili Chutney
  (page 207), for serving
Ketchup, for serving

The constant companion to all the burgers and bun kababs at Zareen's, and a popular standalone act especially among our young and young-at-heart customers, these savory fries are a simple but potent comfort food to have at any time and with nearly any main.

▼▼▼▼▼▼▼▼▼▼▼▼▼▼▼▼▼▼▼▼▼▼▼▼▼▼

* In a karahi, wok, or deep pot, heat 2 inches of oil over medium heat until the oil reaches 350 degrees F.

* Deep-fry the french fries until golden brown and crisp, 5 to 6 minutes.

* Remove the fries with a slotted spatula and place them in a large paper-towel-lined bowl to remove excess oil.

* Sprinkle generously with chaat masala, and toss to nicely coat the fries.

* Serve hot and crispy with a side of red hot garlic-chili chutney and ketchup.

DESI-STYLE CHICKEN CORN SOUP

Pakistani-Chinese Chicken Egg Drop Soup

For the broth:
4 chicken drumsticks
  or thighs
½ medium onion
1 (2-inch) piece ginger
4 garlic cloves
6 black peppercorns

8 tablespoons cornstarch
1 (8.25-ounce) can cream-
  style corn
1 egg white, beaten
1 teaspoon salt (or to taste)
½ teaspoon freshly ground
  black pepper
Sriracha, for serving
2 teaspoons chopped
  green onions
Chili Vinegar (recipe
  follows), for serving

PRO TIP

In a hurry? Use store-bought broth or Knorr Chicken Cubes—it won't be the same as homemade broth, but it's much less effort.

This is such a nostalgic favorite for the Pakistani abroad. Dinner at a Chinese restaurant on Tariq Road was always a treat and the opening salvo was always chicken corn soup, with its thick and velvety broth, creamy egg drop, golden sweet corn, and tender chicken morsels. Enjoy the soup from this recipe with a dash of your favorite red chili sauce. We prefer sriracha and a few drops of green-chili-infused vinegar.

▼▼▼▼▼▼▼▼▼▼▼▼▼▼▼▼▼▼▼▼▼▼▼▼▼▼

MAKE THE BROTH:

- In a large pot, boil all the broth ingredients with 10 cups of water on medium low for about 45 minutes.

- Strain the broth and meat from the other ingredients and set aside the broth. You should have about 7 cups of broth; you will need 6½ cups for this recipe.

- Remove the chicken meat from the bones, shred, and set aside in a small bowl for later use; you should have about 1 cup of chicken meat.

- In a bowl, whisk the cornstarch and 1½ cup of room temperature (not warm!) chicken broth to make a smooth broth-and-cornstarch slurry. Set aside.

- In a deep pot, add 5 cups of the chicken broth, the chicken, and corn, and heat over high heat until the mixture comes to a boil.

- Turn down the heat to medium low, and slowly stir in the broth-and-cornstarch slurry. Keep stirring until the mixture thickens to the desired consistency, about 2 to 3 minutes.

- Reduce the heat to a simmer and slowly stir in the egg. Keep stirring gently for another minute or so to make egg ribbons.

- Add the salt and pepper, adjusting to taste. Keep the pot on simmer until ready to serve. This will prevent the soup from becoming runny.

- Serve in four individual soup bowls with a dash of sriracha, a garnish of about ½ teaspoon green onions per bowl, and a few drops of chili vinegar.

CONTINUED

Chili Vinegar

½ cup white vinegar
2 tablespoons finely
   chopped serrano or Thai
   chilies, deseed chilies if
   you prefer a mild vinegar
½ teaspoon salt (or to taste)
¼ teaspoon sugar

+ In a clean glass bowl, mix all the ingredients.

+ Microwave for about 45 seconds.

+ Let chilies steep for 15 to 20 minutes before serving.

+ Store in an airtight jar in the fridge. Since vinegar is a preservative, this chili-infused vinegar keeps for a month in the fridge.

YAKHNI
Spicy Chicken Broth

For the broth:
1 whole chicken, skinned
    and quartered
½ cup roughly chopped fresh
    cilantro including stalks
1 tablespoon chopped ginger
1 tablespoon coriander seeds
1 teaspoon cumin seeds
2 to 3 teaspoons salt
1 teaspoon cayenne red chili
    powder (optional)
½ teaspoon ground turmeric
½ teaspoon black
    peppercorns
6 to 8 garlic cloves or
    1 tablespoon garlic paste
4 to 5 whole cloves
1 small cinnamon stick or
    to taste
1 bell pepper, cut into large
    pieces
1 large carrot, sliced into
    large pieces
2 to 3 serrano or jalapeño
    peppers (optional)
1 large onion, coarsely
    chopped
5 medium Roma tomatoes
    or 3 large beefsteak toma-
    toes, coarsely chopped
1 lemongrass stalk (optional)

For serving:
Freshly squeezed lemon juice
Freshly ground black pepper

A steaming bowl of yakhni, Pakistan's take on chicken broth, is the perfect preface to any meal and a popular fix for colds and flu. Our recipe gets its heat from both serrano peppers and cayenne chili powder: feel free to adjust or eliminate either to dial the heat level down. Fans of Instant Pot will be happy to hear that we get the best results when we make yakhni using our Instant Pot at home.

▾▾▾▾▾▾▾▾▾▾▾▾▾▾▾▾▾▾▾▾▾▾▾▾▾▾▾▾▾

PRO TIPS

Yakhni keeps well in the fridge for 3 to 4 days.

Besides being added back into the broth, the boiled chicken meat is perfect for salads and sandwiches, and stores well for 2 days in the fridge.

MAKE THE BROTH PHASE 1:

- In a large pot or an Instant Pot on the "Soup" setting, add the chicken and all other broth ingredients with enough water to submerge the chicken quarters. Bring to a boil and let cook on low-medium heat for about 1 hour.

- After 1 hour, while the rest of the broth continues to simmer, remove the chicken quarters from the pot, place in a dish, and let them cool for a few minutes.

- Remove the chicken meat from the bones, shred, and store in the fridge.

MAKE THE BROTH PHASE 2:

- Put the bones back in the simmering broth; top up with more water to cover if needed. Cook on low heat for another 2 hours.

- Strain the broth into a large container. Remove and discard bones. Cool and store broth in the fridge until ready to serve. Before serving, reheat broth.

FOR EACH INDIVIDUAL SERVING:

- Pour 2 cups of hot broth into each soup bowl.

- Add ¼ cup boiled and shredded chicken.

- Add a dash of lemon juice.

- Sprinkle with pepper.

II.

NAASHTA

•••••••••••••••••••••

Breakfast
and Brunch

MASALA OMELET Ⓥ

Traditional Pakistani Omelet

6 eggs

⅓ cup finely chopped onion

¼ cup chopped fresh cilantro, plus more for garnish

1 serrano chili, finely chopped (deseed for less heat)

½ medium tomato, finely chopped

¼ to ½ teaspoon cayenne red chili powder (optional)

½ teaspoon salt (or to taste)

1 tablespoon milk (optional)

3 to 4 tablespoons ghee or oil, divided

PRO TIP

You can add other chopped vegetables, such as bell pepper, mushroom, other herbs, like mint, and cheese, per personal preference.

The three mandatory ingredients in a Pakistani omelet are onions, fresh cilantro, and green chilies. You can deseed the green chilies but you cannot skip them. We add chopped tomatoes as well. The overall appearance and texture is that of a golden-brown American-style omelet.

Enjoy with Paratha (page 184), Roti (page 181), sweet challah bread, or toasted sourdough, or encase in a toasted bagel or crusty baguette in the company of cheese, avocado, and Japanese mayonnaise for a mean breakfast sandwich. The Masala Omelet is also the most common centerpiece of the Anda Paratha Qeema (page 88) brunch.

▼▼▼▼▼▼▼▼▼▼▼▼▼▼▼▼▼▼▼▼▼▼▼▼▼▼▼

• Crack the eggs into a medium bowl and beat with a fork until well mixed but not too frothy. Add the onion, cilantro, chilies, tomato, cayenne, milk, and salt, and beat the mixture well.

• In a medium skillet, heat half of the ghee over medium heat. Pour half of the egg mixture into the pan and fry until eggs begin to set, about 30 to 45 seconds. Then use a spatula to lift the eggs while tipping the skillet, to let the uncooked eggs run underneath, until the eggs set, about 45 seconds.

• Use a spatula to flip the omelet and cook for another 30 to 45 seconds on the other side. Fold the omelet and slide it onto a plate.

• Fry the remaining egg mixture in the remaining ghee to make a second omelet.

• Garnish the omelets with chopped cilantro and enjoy with your bread of choice.

KHAGEENA ⓥ
Spiced Egg Scramble

6 eggs

2 tablespoons milk

¾ teaspoon salt

¼ cup ghee or oil

½ cup onion, finely chopped

2 medium tomatoes, finely
chopped

1½ serrano chilies, finely
chopped, deseed for
less heat

½ teaspoon cayenne red
chili powder

¼ teaspoon ground turmeric

⅓ cup chopped fresh cilantro, plus more for garnish

¼ teaspoon freshly ground
black pepper (optional)

PRO TIP

You can make a large batch
of the spicy onion-tomato
masala base and store it in
the fridge for up to 12 hours,
until ready to serve. When
ready to make Khageena,
simply reheat the masala
in a pan and add the egg
mixture.

"When in doubt, add spice." Applying this unofficial national motto to the American egg scramble, Pakistanis give you Khageena. A perfect breakfast entree on its own, it is also a delicious base for your favorite hipster toppings such as ripe avocado or artisanal cheese.

Khageena is most commonly enjoyed in Pakistan with a Paratha (page 184), Puri (page 197), or Roti (page 181), often taking the egg spot in the Anda Paratha Qeema (page 88) breakfast. It is commonly enjoyed by us Desi Californians with a buttered slice of toasted San Francisco sourdough and Doodh Patti Chai (page 225).

▾▾▾▾▾▾▾▾▾▾▾▾▾▾▾▾▾▾▾▾▾▾▾▾▾

- In a medium bowl, add the eggs, milk, and salt. Whisk and set aside.

- In a large, nonstick frying pan, heat the ghee over medium heat.

- Add the onion to the pan; sauté until the onion turns translucent. Don't overcook and brown the onion.

- Add the tomatoes and serrano chilies to the pan and sauté until the tomatoes soften, 4 to 5 minutes.

- Add the cayenne, turmeric, and cilantro, stir, and sauté for another 2 minutes. The onion-tomato "masala" base for your eggs is now ready.

- Add the egg mixture to the pan. Stir for 3 minutes over medium-low heat until the eggs are cooked.

- Sprinkle with pepper, garnish with fresh cilantro, and serve. Enjoy with roti, paratha, or buttered toast.

HALWA PURI NASHTA WITH ALOO BHUJIA AND CHOLAY ⓥ

Traditional Pakistani Breakfast Platter

1 recipe Puri (page 197)
1 recipe Aloo Bhujia (recipe follows)
1 recipe Lahori Cholay (page 162)
1 recipe Sooji Halwa (page 241)
Memoni Carrot Achar (page 212) or store-bought

The breakfast of champions: a platter of sweet sooji halwa, aloo bhujia, cholay, and puris. Sooji halwa is a traditional Pakistani confection consisting of semolina flour, sugar, and various flavors and essences fried in ghee (or oil). At breakfast, it is accompanied by puffed-up puris. This composite recipe simply requires assembly once you have the components.

▾▾▾▾▾▾▾▾▾▾▾▾▾▾▾▾▾▾▾▾▾▾▾▾▾▾

TO SERVE FAMILY STYLE:

• Place the puris on a *thali* platter and put the aloo bhujia, lahori cholay, and sooji halwa in serving bowls.

TO SERVE INDIVIDUALLY:

• On a large *thali* place two puris and one serving each of aloo bhujia, lahori cholay, and sooji halwa. Accompany with Memoni carrot achar.

ALOO BHUJIA ⓥ

Potato Stew

1 pound (about 3 medium) potatoes, peeled and cut into 1-inch pieces
2 tablespoons oil
1 teaspoon salt (or to taste)
1 teaspoon red pepper flakes
1 teaspoon ground coriander
½ teaspoon ground turmeric
½ teaspoon nigella seeds
½ tablespoon store-bought raw mango achar (pickle), or to taste

The must-have savory element in any halwa puri breakfast, aloo bhujia is also a popular side at lunch or dinner next to a meat main.

▾▾▾▾▾▾▾▾▾▾▾▾▾▾▾▾▾▾▾▾▾▾▾▾▾▾

• In a large saucepan, add about 2 ½ cups of water, the potatoes, oil, salt, spices, and nigella seeds.

• Bring to a boil, then lower heat and cook on medium for 15 to 20 minutes, stirring occasionally, until the potatoes are cooked through and become soft.

• With a wooden spoon, mash some of the potatoes to thicken the sauce. Mix in mango achar, stir, and serve hot.

ANDA PARATHA QEEMA

Eggs, Paratha, and Spicy Ground Beef

2 recipes Masala Omelet
   (page 82) or 2 recipes
   Khageena (page 83)
1 recipe Paratha (page 184);
   4 parathas or Lachha
   Paratha (page 189)
1 recipe Aloo Qeema or Pea
   Qeema (page 121)
Kachumar (page 208), for
   serving
Hari Chutney (page 205),
   for serving

The classic breakfast combination of eggs-bread-meat done Pakistani style. Another composite brunch, this is a worthy competitor to Halwa Puri (page 87) and one that significantly ups the protein content of its rival. Usually reserved for a weekend brunch, it is nevertheless easy to make if a suitable dish is left over from the night before and roti is substituted for the slightly more time-consuming paratha or use ready-to-fry store-bought parathas.

The qeema spicy ground beef can be replaced with your favorite kabab such as Chapli Kabab (page 129) or Gola Kabab (page 126). A vegetarian version of this breakfast featuring Aloo Tikki (page 151) is very popular at Zareen's.

▾▾▾▾▾▾▾▾▾▾▾▾▾▾▾▾▾▾▾▾▾▾▾▾▾▾

TO SERVE FAMILY STYLE:

* Plate the omelets, place the parathas on a platter, and put the aloo qeema in a serving bowl.

TO SERVE INDIVIDUALLY:

* On a large plate, put an omelet, a hot paratha, and a generous portion of aloo qeema.

* Accompany with kachumar and hari chutney.

III.

MURGH

❖•❖•❖•❖•❖•❖•❖•❖•❖

Mainly Chicken

ON KARAHI CHICKEN

If Italian cacciatore and Chinese stir-fry had a gifted child that trained in culinary combat in the rugged north of Pakistan, the brawny, belligerent prodigy would be karahi chicken.

In a large karahi Pakistani wok, heat a hair-raising amount of ghee to fry up bone-in chicken, an excess of ripe tomatoes, far too many green chilies, large dollops of garlic, and other loud spices. Simmer this stew to release every ounce of bone broth, and cook until you see the tawny glow of risen ghee. Lash liberally with garam masala, more green chilies, fresh coriander, and ginger strands. Leave your best porcelain in the cabinet and always serve this specialty in the heavy metal karahi where it was forged, alongside scalding hot naan or roti.

There are some Pakistani specialties that are best enjoyed at local restaurants and others that are best when made at home. Very few transcend this divide. Karahi chicken is one.

KARAHI CHICKEN

¾ cup oil

1 whole medium chicken, cut up into 14 to 16 small pieces

1 tablespoon garlic paste

1 tablespoon ginger paste

½ tablespoon red pepper flakes

2 teaspoons salt (or to taste)

1 tablespoon coriander powder

1 teaspoon cayenne red chili powder (optional)

½ teaspoon ground turmeric

3 medium tomatoes, coarsely chopped

2 tablespoons tomato paste

3 tablespoons plain yogurt

3 to 4 whole green chilies per taste preference

1 teaspoon dried fenugreek leaves (optional)

2 tablespoons unsalted butter (optional)

2 tablespoons julienned ginger

2 tablespoons freshly squeezed lemon or lime juice

½ to 1 teaspoon coarsely ground black pepper, to taste

½ teaspoon Garam Masala (page 215)

¼ cup chopped fresh cilantro

Naans or rotis, for serving

PRO TIPS

Instead of a whole chicken, you can use 8 pieces of bone-in chicken thighs or 8 drumsticks. Or use 2 pounds of boneless chicken thighs (you will miss out on the richness of bone broth). To increase the heat, top with sliced green chilies.

In this robust subcontinental stew, tomatoes, bone broth, fresh ginger, and green chilies are the stars of the show. Small pieces of bone-in chicken are key to getting maximum bone broth flavor; using large pieces chicken quarters or going boneless, while not ideal, is acceptable if more convenient.

Karahi chicken is the starring dish at any meal so never pair it with another main unless it is a truly grand occasion. Tarka Daal (page 159) or Aloo Palak (page 147) make excellent menu mates. While typically served with Sesame Seed Naan (page 193) or Roti (page 181), it pairs well with Plain White Basmati Rice (page 168) too. Typically, no raitas, chutney, pickles, or other flavorful condiments are needed. A refreshing side of Kachumar (page 208) or a dollop of plain yogurt to ease the heat are usually welcome.

▾▾▾▾▾▾▾▾▾▾▾▾▾▾▾▾▾▾▾▾▾▾▾▾▾▾▾▾

• In a large karahi or wok, heat the oil over medium-high heat.

• Add the chicken pieces and fry until golden brown, 8 to 10 minutes.

• Add garlic and ginger paste and cook for about 1 to 2 minutes.

• Add the red pepper flakes, salt, coriander, cayenne (optional), turmeric, tomatoes, and tomato paste, and sauté for 2 to 3 minutes, stirring regularly.

• Add ½ cup of water and cook on medium heat for about 10 minutes until the chicken is done, checking and stirring occasionally. Add a splash of water if the sauce appears to stick to the karahi.

• In a cup, add the yogurt with 2 tablespoons of water and use a fork to whip until smooth.

• Add the yogurt, green chilies, and fenugreek leaves to the karahi.

• Over low-medium heat, continue to cook and stir for 8 to 10 minutes, until the oil separates (the bhunna process, see page 49).

• Add the butter and give a quick stir, then sprinkle in the ginger, lemon juice, black pepper, and garam masala. Garnish with the cilantro. Cover and remove from heat.

• Serve in the karahi with hot naans or rotis on the side.

MEMONI CRISPY FRIED CHICKEN

For the marinated chicken:
1 small whole chicken
   (3 pounds), cut into
   8 pieces (or 3 pounds
   bone-in chicken thighs or
   drumsticks)
6 to 8 Thai green chilies
½ cup loosely packed fresh
   cilantro, chopped
½ cup plain yogurt
3 tablespoons white vinegar
1 tablespoon ginger paste
1 tablespoon garlic paste
1½ teaspoons salt
1 teaspoon ground cumin
2 teaspoons Garam Masala
   (page 215)

For the batter:
2 eggs
2 cups panko bread crumbs
Oil, for frying
Chaat Masala (page 214),
   for serving
Garlic-Chili Ketchup (page
   207), for serving (optional)
Wicked Spicy Chutney
   (page 207) or another
   favorite chutney, for
   serving (optional)

I remember having this green masala-infused crispy chicken as a child. My mom would serve these chicken pieces next to a heap of french fries with a side of spicy ketchup on especially lucky afternoons. Prickly-crunchy outside and tender inside—and yes, I am talking about the fried chicken, not the cook—this was the ultimate comfort food after a long day at school. Try this with our Masala Fries (page 75) or Karachi-Style Coleslaw (page 209).

▼▼▼▼▼▼▼▼▼▼▼▼▼▼▼▼▼▼▼▼▼▼▼▼▼▼

PRO TIPS

The ready-to-fry chicken freezes really well. After cooking and coating the chicken pieces, line them on a baking sheet and put in the freezer for a few hours. When frozen-hard, pack them in a freezer bag and store. When ready to use, defrost and fry.

I love the fragrance and flavor of Thai chilies, but you can always substitute with other less potent green chilies like serrano or jalapeño.

In this recipe, you can use a small, whole chicken cut into 8 to 10 pieces, or a 3 pound package of bone-in chicken thighs or drumsticks.

Yogurt creates an acidic medium for the spices and helps tenderize the chicken so that flavors can penetrate into the meat.

Want to forgo the frying? Spray the panko-coated pieces with olive oil and place on a nonstick oiled baking sheet. Bake at 400 degrees F for about 20 minutes until golden and crispy.

• Wash and drain the chicken and set aside in a glass bowl.

• In a blender, combine the chilies, cilantro, yogurt, vinegar, ginger, garlic, salt, cumin, and garam masala, and blend to make a smooth marinade.

• Pour the marinade over the chicken and toss so the chicken is evenly coated. Marinate the chicken for at least 1 hour but preferably for 2 or more hours.

CONTINUED

- In a wide saucepan over medium-low heat, cook the marinated chicken, stirring occasionally, until the masala thickens and clings to the chicken, about 30 to 40 minutes. At this point, almost all liquid should have dried up and the masala should be clinging to the chicken pieces.

- In a medium bowl, whisk the eggs and 2 tablespoons water to make an egg wash.

- Pour the panko out onto a wide platter. Pat the masala around the chicken pieces to ensure the masala clings to the chicken. Now dredge the chicken pieces, one at a time, in the egg wash and then coat each piece with panko. Set all the pieces on a baking sheet until ready for frying.

- In a karahi, wok, or deep frying pan, heat 2 to 3 inches of oil over medium-high heat.

- When the oil is hot (350 degrees F) and ready for deep-frying per the wooden spoon test, see (page 32), put the chicken pieces, a few at time, into the oil. Don't overcrowd the pan.

- Turn the heat to medium and cook until golden brown. It takes only a few minutes as the chicken is already cooked.

- Sprinkle a few pinches of chaat masala over the chicken pieces and serve immediately, accompanied with garlic-chili ketchup and wicked spicy chutney.

GRILLED CHICKEN BOTI

For the marinade:

3 tablespoons oil
¼ cup freshly squeezed
    lemon or lime juice
3 tablespoons Greek yogurt
2 tablespoons paprika
2 teaspoons cayenne red
    chili powder
2 teaspoons garlic paste
1 teaspoon crushed corian-
    der seeds
1½ teaspoons salt
3 tablespoons white vinegar
½ teaspoon cumin powder
½ teaspoon freshly ground
    black pepper
1 tablespoon mashed fresh
    papaya
¼ teaspoon Garam Masala
    (page 215)

2 pounds boneless chicken
    thighs, cut into 2-inch
    strips
2 tablespoons oil
1 small onion, sliced
¼ cup chopped fresh
    cilantro
Sliced green chilies
    (optional)
Lemon wedges, for serving
Hari Chutney (page 205), for
    serving

Arguably the most popular dish at our restaurant, Zareen's grilled chicken boti is served sizzling on heated cast-iron platters. This recipe translates our star dish for home cooks, making it a little less theatrical but no less mouthwatering.

Besides headlining at any meal, chicken boti is also a delectable filling in Paratha Rolls (page 73) and is the main ingredient in our Chicken Tikka Masala (page 105). It is also the perfect protein to top any salad, such as our hugely popular Desi Paleo Salad (page 66).

▼▼▼▼▼▼▼▼▼▼▼▼▼▼▼▼▼▼▼▼▼▼▼▼▼▼▼

- In a large bowl, thoroughly mix all the marinade ingredients.

- Add the chicken thighs and toss to evenly coat the pieces. Let them rest for 30 to 60 minutes.

- Grill or barbecue the marinated chicken pieces for 12 to 14 minutes, turning once midway through grilling, until the chicken reaches an internal temperature of 165 degrees F and is done, i.e., juice no longer runs pink when cutting into the thickest part of the meat. Alternatively, on a greased baking sheet in the oven, broil the chicken on high, without turning, until the chicken reaches an internal temperature of 165 degrees F and is done. Set aside.

- Add the oil to a small frying pan and sauté the onion over medium heat until sweet and translucent, not brown, about 2 minutes.

- Serve the grilled chicken with sauteed onions and garnish with cilantro and green chilies. Serve with lemon wedges and hari chutney on the side.

ON HALEEM

Burns Road, Karachi, is a few blocks of aging Victorian buildings perfect for watching humanity go past on overloaded motorcycles and rickshaws. It is also the greatest food street in the world.

Among its culinary crown jewels are the restaurants Karachi Haleem and Mazaidar Haleem. If you can make your way past the street stalls and double-parked vehicles up front, you will find each to be a clean, well-lit place to enjoy the best plateful of haleem in Asia.

Haleem is a Mughal-era mashup of rich meat korma and spicy lentil-n-grains porridge. Meat beef, mutton, or chicken, spices, lentils, barley, and wheat are simmered and hand-churned for long hours in large cauldrons until the golden yellow viscosity of great haleem is forged.

Order a "double plate:" a "single" is a delusional overestimate of your self-control. Your plate of steaming haleem will come with six toppings. A liberal scattering of crisp-caramelized onions and fresh cilantro, a more measured sprinkling of finely chopped green chilies and julienned ginger, a squeeze of lemon, and a dash of chaat masala. Give it a quick stir, and you are ready for your first bite.

Haleem is best eaten neat by the spoonful but there is joy, too, in scooping it up with blistering hot naan. The steaming textures and the sultry night air will lead to a sweaty euphoria—and a life-long addiction.

CHICKEN HALEEM
Meat, Lentil, and Grain Stew

For the lentil and grain porridge:
⅓ cup split Bengal gram (chana daal)
¼ cup split white lentils (urad)
½ cup haleem wheat
3 tablespoons pearl barley
1 ½ teaspoons salt

For the chicken stew:
½ cup ghee or oil
1 tablespoon ginger paste
1 tablespoon garlic paste
1¼ pounds chicken breast, cut into large chunks
1½ tablespoon ground coriander
1 teaspoon ground cumin
1½ tablespoons Garam Masala (page 215)
1 teaspoon ground turmeric
1½ teaspoons cayenne red chili powder

For the tarka:
¼ cup oil
1 medium onion, thinly sliced

For the garnish:
1 (1-inch) piece ginger, peeled and thinly julienned
1 lemon, sliced
2 tablespoons chopped fresh cilantro
1 teaspoon Chaat Masala (page 214)
2 serrano chilies, finely chopped

Like preparing nihari, making haleem for family and friends is a true test of one's devotion. Take heart, our method foregoes hours of hand-churning in favor of speedy whisks and blenders, while keeping all ingredients and flavors intact. An all-in-one protein, grain, and fat extravaganza, haleem is best eaten neat or with the aid of Naan (page 193) or Roti (page 181). Beef haleem is the most popular version, but chicken haleem has gained its acolytes as well; in our household it is the favorite. See Pro Tips for guidance on substituting beef or lamb.

▼▼▼▼▼▼▼▼▼▼▼▼▼▼▼▼▼▼▼▼▼▼▼▼▼▼▼

PRO TIPS

Bulgur wheat can be substituted for haleem wheat.

If you substitute chicken with boneless beef or lamb, use stew meat, add another 2 to 3 cups of water when cooking the meat stew in step 2, and allow another 30 to 45 minutes for the meat to get fork tender.

MAKE THE LENTIL AND GRAIN PORRIDGE:

• Wash the lentils and grains and soak in water for a few hours or overnight. Drain.

• In a Dutch oven, add about 7 cups of water and add in the drained lentils and grains.

• Bring to a full boil for a few minutes and then cook on low for 50 to 60 minutes or until completely soft. Add in more water to cook longer, if needed. Add salt and mix.

• Using an immersion blender or a regular blender if you don't have an immersion blender, blend until smooth. Add hot water if it's too thick. The consistency should be that of a thin porridge.

MAKE THE CHICKEN STEW:

• In a large Dutch oven over medium heat, heat the ghee, then add the ginger, garlic, chicken, and all the chicken stew spices, and fry for 1 to 2 minutes.

- Add in ½ cup of water to ensure the spices don't burn. Cook on medium, stirring frequently, for 10 to 12 minutes until the spices are cooked and the water is almost dried up (the bhunna process, see page 49).

- Now add in 3 cups of water, cover, and cook on medium low until the chicken is fork tender, 20 to 25 minutes, and a thick sauce remains. Turn off the heat.

- Using an electric hand mixer, shred the stewed chicken finely. If you do not have a hand mixer, shred the chicken using a fork. *Do not* use an immersion blender at this stage, otherwise the chicken meat will be ground too fine and no strands will remain to give your dish the unique haleem texture.

- Add the lentil and grain porridge to the chicken stew and stir well.

- Turn the heat back on to low, cover, and simmer until ready to add the tarka tempered oil.

MAKE THE TARKA:

- In a frying pan, heat the oil and onion, and fry until the onions are golden brown.

- Set aside 2 tablespoons of fried onion and put the rest of the fried onion along with the hot oil on top of the haleem and cover with a lid.

- When ready to serve, give the haleem a gentle stir and ladle into a large serving bowl or casserole dish.

- Garnish with the reserved fried onions, the ginger, lemon slices, cilantro, and chaat masala. Place the chilies on the side allowing diners to top their serving of haleem, if they choose.

CHICKEN TIKKA MASALA

For the tikka masala sauce:

1 large onion, sliced

¼ cup oil

2 teaspoons ginger paste

2 teaspoons garlic paste

2 large tomatoes, chopped

2 tablespoons tomato paste

1 tablespoon ground coriander

½ tablespoon sugar (or to taste)

1 teaspoon salt

1 tablespoon paprika

1 teaspoon Garam Masala (page 215)

1 teaspoon cayenne red chili powder

½ teaspoon ground turmeric

½ stick (¼ cup) unsalted butter

1 cup plus 1 teaspoon heavy cream, divided

1 tablespoon freshly squeezed lemon juice

1 tablespoon dried fenugreek leaves

1 recipe Grilled Chicken Boti (page 99)

1 tablespoon finely chopped fresh cilantro

Pinch of Garam Masala

The most famous instance of the fusion of English and sub-continental cuisines, chicken tikka masala is the gateway drug at Zareen's for all newcomers to Pakistani food, thanks in large part to its mild spice levels and creamy, velvety texture. Best enjoyed with Garlic Naan (page 193), it is equally satisfying atop Aromatic Yellow Rice (page 170).

Our recipe reveals the art of making the perfect tikka masala sauce. This is combined with Grilled Chicken Boti (page 99) to create the ultimate Chicken Tikka Masala.

▼▼▼▼▼▼▼▼▼▼▼▼▼▼▼▼▼▼▼▼▼▼▼▼▼▼▼▼

MAKE THE TIKKA MASALA SAUCE:

- In a medium saucepan, fry the onion in the oil over medium heat until golden brown, 8 to 10 minutes.

- Add the ginger and garlic and stir-fry for 1 minute.

- Add the tomatoes, tomato paste, coriander, sugar, salt, paprika, garam masala, cayenne, turmeric, and butter, and cook on medium-low heat, stirring frequently, for 8 to 10 minutes, until the oil rises, stirring occasionally, and mashing the tomatoes, for about 25 minutes until the sauce thickens to a gravy consistency.

- Turn off the heat. Transfer mixture from saucepan to a blender and blend until smooth. For a smoother consistency, strain the mixture through a sieve. Return to saucepan.

- Bring the saucepan back to the stove. Add 1 cup of cream, ½ cup water, lemon juice, and dried fenugreek leaves, and cook on low heat to desired consistency, about 15 minutes. Don't overheat the sauce as the cream will separate.

- Chop the grilled chicken boti into bite-size pieces and add to the tikka masala sauce. Mix, and let simmer for 3 to 4 minutes.

- To serve, garnish with the cilantro, a sprinkle of garam masala, and the remaining teaspoon of cream.

MADRAS COCONUT CURRY WITH CHICKEN

For the masala paste:

4 tablespoons tomato paste

1 tablespoon curry powder

2 teaspoons ground coriander

2 teaspoons salt (or to taste)

1½ teaspoons cayenne red chili powder

¼ cup ghee or oil

¾ teaspoon black mustard seeds

1 medium onion, thinly sliced

1 tablespoon garlic paste

1 tablespoon ginger paste

1½ pounds boneless chicken thighs, cut into 1-inch cubes

1 medium carrot, cut into 1-inch-thick slices

5 to 6 fingerling potatoes

1 (12-ounce) can unsweetened coconut milk

½ cup frozen peas

½ bell pepper, cut into 1-inch squares

10 to 12 curry leaves (optional)

1 tablespoon freshly squeezed lime or lemon juice

½ teaspoon Garam Masala (page 215)

¼ cup chopped fresh cilantro

1 serrano chili pepper cut lengthwise, for garnish (optional)

Coconut milk does not feature prominently in Pakistani cooking; thankfully some Burmese and Sri Lankan influence made its way through to give a sweet, creamy note to spicy stews and curries. This recipe is based on a crowd favorite at Zareen's and is best served with Plain White Basmati Rice (page 168) and Kachumbar (page 208).

▼▼▼▼▼▼▼▼▼▼▼▼▼▼▼▼▼▼▼▼▼▼▼▼▼

- In a small bowl, mix the tomato paste, 2 to 3 tablespoons of water, curry powder, coriander, salt, and cayenne to make a masala paste.

- In a medium saucepan, heat the ghee over medium heat.

- Add the mustard seeds and stir until the seeds stop popping, about 30 seconds. Take care as the seeds can burn easily.

- Immediately add the onion and sauté until golden, 6 to 8 minutes.

- Add the garlic, ginger, the masala paste, and the chicken, and stir-fry for 3 to 4 minutes. Add ¾ cup of water. Cover and cook on low-medium heat for 30 to 35 minutes, until chicken is fork tender. Add the garlic and ginger and stir-fry for 1 minute.

- Add the carrot and potato. Cover and cook until vegetables are done.

- Reduce the heat to a simmer and then add the coconut milk, peas, bell pepper, and curry leaves. Cook until all vegetables are cooked through, about 5 to 7 minutes.

- To finish, stir in the lime juice and garam masala, and garnish with cilantro and green chilies.

VARIATION ⓥ

MADRAS COCONUT CURRY WITH PANEER AND VEGETABLES: Skip the chicken and replace it with paneer for a home-cooked version of this firm favorite among our vegetarian diners.

Substitute the chicken with two 8-ounce packages of paneer. All other ingredients remain the same. Cut the paneer into 1-inch cubes and set aside. When cooking the carrot and potato, cook until half done, 6 to 8 minutes. Add the paneer when adding the coconut milk, peas, bell pepper, and curry leaves. Cook until all vegetables are cooked through, another 6 to 8 minutes.

ON KHOWSAY

No kitchen is as important to the Karachi childhood as the ethnic kitchen of our favorite aunty. And no aunty is more treasured than the Memon aunty who has perfected the art of khowsay.

Officially, khowsay began as a post–World War II Burmese import into the Karachi Memon community. The unofficial and unfalsifiable theory is that a 1950s Memon aunty time-traveled to Mughal India, Ayutthayan Siam, and Ming China to create a multicultural mash-up featuring bhunna gosht, coconut milk, and noodles.

Your tableside assembly of khowsay starts with a bowl of creamy curry. In the Memoni/Gujrati variant, this is the popular gram-flour-and-yogurt curry called karhi, fortified with spicy green masala and coconut milk. Into this Memoni karhi, add a tong full of noodles. Next up is bhunna gosht, a rich meat stew with masala clinging to tender meat morsels. Take as many servings as you dare under Aunty's watchful gaze. The thick masala will start to swirl into the steaming soup, smear the slippery noodles, and entwine the aromatic fumes rising up around you. Your contemplation of this unfinished work of art is broken when Aunty gestures toward the garnishes before you: crisp-fried onions, fried potato wedges, boiled egg slices, crunchy fried noodles, chopped mint, fresh cilantro, fried garlic slivers, chopped green chilies, red pepper flakes, and lemon wedges. Take some of all. "Everything in moderation" never felt so excessive.

Several steaming spoonfuls later, you, too, shall become eternally grateful to Memon aunties. And you will see why, despite its tendency to occasionally reach a boiling point, Karachi will remain our favorite melting pot, as long as the ethnic aunty remains at its hearth.

MEMONI-STYLE KHOWSAY

Braised Chicken and Noodle
Stew with Garnishes

*For Bombay-style coconut
  yogurt kurhi broth:*
2 cups yogurt
½ cup roughly chopped
  fresh cilantro
1 teaspoon cumin seeds
4 green chilies
4 tablespoons gram flour
1 teaspoon turmeric
1 teaspoon salt
¼ cup oil
½ teaspoon mustard seeds
3 curry leaves (optional)
½ small onion, thinly sliced
1 (12-ounce) can coconut milk

For the kalya:
2 teaspoons ground coriander
1 teaspoon salt (or to taste)
1½ teaspoon ginger paste
1½ teaspoon garlic paste
1 teaspoon cayenne red
  chili powder
½ teaspoon ground turmeric
⅓ cup oil
1 large onion, thinly sliced
3 Roma tomatoes, chopped
  finely
1 tablespoon tomato paste
2 cups boneless chicken
  breast, cut into bite-size
  pieces
1 teaspoon Garam Masala
  (page 215)

A delicious concoction of noodles, spicy chicken, rich broth, and numerous toppings, khowsay is a one-dish meal. Ours is a Memoni take on the legendary Burmese stew, khow suey. We use a popular Pakistani yogurt-and-gram-flour curry as the soup base. Memoni kalya, a braised masala chicken, is served as the main meat topping. Serve this dish family-style, with the noodles, the Bombay-style coconut yogurt kurhi broth, and the kalya in separate serving dishes, and the garnishes in small bowls. Pass out large shallow bowls for each diner to help themselves.

MAKE THE BOMBAY-STYLE COCONUT YOGURT KURHI BROTH:

* In a blender, blend the yogurt with the cilantro, cumin seeds, and green chilies.

* To the yogurt mixture, add 2 cups of water, gram flour, the turmeric, and salt, and blend again until smooth. Set aside.

* In a medium saucepan, heat the oil over medium heat.

* Add the mustard seeds and let them sizzle for 30 seconds.

* Add the curry leaves and onion, and fry for about 2 minutes until the onion turns translucent.

* Add the yogurt mixture slowly and stir frequently. It is important to keep stirring until the mixture starts to boil, to prevent the yogurt from curdling.

* Turn the heat to low and let the curry simmer for about 15 to 20 minutes.

* Add the coconut milk, simmer for about 5 minutes, and then turn off the heat. Keep warm until ready to serve.

MAKE THE KALYA:

* In a small bowl, add 4 tablespoons of water, the coriander, salt, ginger, garlic, cayenne, and turmeric, and mix to form a masala paste. Set aside.

CONTINUED

For the noodles:

1 package spaghetti, cooked according to package directions, drained, and tossed in 2 tablespoons olive oil

For the garnish:

CRUNCHY: fried slivered garlic, crispy fried onions, or hand-crushed Pakistani chili chips; substitute with other spicy potato chips like spicy Doritos or Pringles

SPICY: red pepper flakes

TANGY: lemon wedges

SAVORY: boiled egg slices

HERBY: chopped fresh mint

OPTIONAL: chopped green onions, chopped fresh cilantro, roasted peanuts, finely sliced green chilies

- In a medium saucepan, heat the oil over medium heat and fry the onion until just golden brown, 10 to 12 minutes.

- Add the masala paste and 2 tablespoons of water and fry well for 2 minutes.

- Add the tomatoes and tomato paste and fry for 1 to 2 minutes, adding a splash of water if the masala sticks to the pan.

- Add the chicken, stir-fry on medium heat for 1 minute, then add 1 cup of water and cook until the chicken is tender and the sauce is nice and thick, about 20 minutes.

- Sprinkle the garam masala on top, cover, and turn off the heat. Set aside until ready to assemble the khowsay.

SERVING KHOWSAY:

- In separate serving dishes, set out the Bombay-style coconut yogurt kurhi broth, the kalya, and the noodles.

- Set out all the garnishes in small bowls.

- Pass out large shallow bowls to diners to help themselves to the three mains and the numerous garnishes of khowsay.

SPICY CHICKEN MANCHURIAN

For the marinade:

1 egg
2 tablespoons cornstarch
   (or to taste)
1 teaspoon toasted sesame
   seed oil
½ teaspoon salt
½ teaspoon freshly ground
   black pepper
¼ teaspoon baking soda

For the Manchurian sauce:
½ cup ketchup
2 tablespoons Chinese chili
   sauce
2 tablespoons soy sauce
1 chicken bouillon cube,
   e.g. Knorr
1 tablespoon vinegar
1 tablespoon sugar
½ teaspoon salt (or to taste)

1 pound chicken breast, cut
   in bite-size chunks
½ cup oil
1 tablespoon minced garlic
1 medium bell pepper, cut
   into 1-inch squares
1 small onion, cut into 1-inch
   squares
1 tablespoon cornstarch
   mixed in ½ cup water
3 green onions, finely sliced
Jasmine rice, for serving

This is a traditional Chinese dish prepared with aromatic Indo-Pak flavors and spices. It is easy to prepare and addictively delicious. Chicken Manchurian is best served alongside fragrant jasmine rice.

▼▼▼▼▼▼▼▼▼▼▼▼▼▼▼▼▼▼▼▼▼▼▼▼▼▼▼▼

- In a small bowl, whisk all the marinade ingredients together.

- Rub the chicken with the marinade and set aside for 15 to 30 minutes.

- In a small bowl, mix all the Manchurian sauce ingredients together and set aside.

- In a wok over medium-high heat, heat the oil and fry the marinated chicken until golden brown and cooked through, 6 to 8 minutes. Take the chicken out with a slotted spoon and set aside.

- In the same wok, stir-fry the garlic over high heat for about 30 seconds. Add the bell pepper and onion, and stir-fry for another 30 seconds.

- Lower the heat to medium and add in the prepared Manchurian sauce. Cook for 2 to 3 minutes, until heated through.

- Add in the cornstarch and water mixture slowly, mixing gently, and cook until the sauce thickens, 2 to 3 minutes.

- Add the cooked chicken back in and cook until heated through, 2 to 3 minutes.

- Garnish with green onions and serve hot with jasmine rice.

POMEGRANATE–GARLIC ROAST CHICKEN WITH GRAVY

For the chicken:

1 whole chicken

1 head of garlic

3 sprigs of rosemary or thyme

3 tablespoons pomegranate molasses, for basting

3 sprigs of thyme or parsley (optional)

Lemon slices, for garnish (optional)

For the marinade:

¼ cup garlic paste

¼ cup pomegranate molasses/concentrate

3 tablespoons olive oil

2 teaspoons salt (or to taste)

2 teaspoons Garam Masala (page 215)

1 teaspoon cayenne red chili powder or paprika for less heat

For the gravy:

⅓ cup cold water, plus more as needed

2 tablespoons cornstarch

Every morsel of this tender roast chicken evokes ripe pomegranates; every bite of its crackling skin speaks of the fresh garlic rub. Pair this upscale Pakistani take on the American classic with the usual American fixings like mashed potatoes or go full South Asian with Zeera Aloo (page 154), Matar Pulao (page 172), and a few Raitas (page 201) and chutneys.

▾▾▾▾▾▾▾▾▾▾▾▾▾▾▾▾▾▾▾▾▾▾▾▾▾▾

MAKE THE CHICKEN:

- Rinse the chicken and pat dry with a paper towel.

- Insert the garlic head and rosemary into the chicken cavity.

MAKE THE MARINADE:

- In a small bowl, mix together all the marinade ingredients.

- Rub the marinade all over the chicken and inside the cavity. Let the chicken marinate for 1 to 2 hours or overnight in the fridge.

- Preheat oven to 350 degrees F.

- Place the chicken on a roasting pan with a rack. Place pan on the center rack of the oven. Bake the chicken for 60 to 80 minutes, basting every 15 minutes with pomegranate molasses. Test doneness by sticking a knife into the drumstick area: if the juices run clear, it is done. Otherwise leave longer in the oven. If using a food thermometer, cook until thigh temperature reads 165 degrees F. If the chicken is browning too fast, tent the chicken with foil or lower the oven temperature.

- When the chicken is done, remove and cover the chicken for 10 minutes, letting it rest before carving.

MAKE THE GRAVY:

- Drain the juices from the roasting pan into a small saucepan. Cook over medium heat, skimming any fat off the top.

- In a small bowl, mix together the cold water and cornstarch, and stir into the stock, a little at a time, whisking constantly. Stop when you reach the desired thickness.

- Taste the gravy and adjust the seasoning and consistency if needed by adding more water, salt, or more juices from the pan.

- Serve the gravy alongside the chicken on a platter, garnished with thyme and lemon slices.

IV.

GOSHT

❖·❖·❖·❖·❖·❖·❖·❖·❖·❖·❖·❖

Meaty Mains

ON ALOO GOSHT

❖◆❖◆❖◆❖◆❖◆❖◆❖◆❖◆❖◆❖◆❖◆❖◆❖◆❖◆❖◆❖◆❖◆❖◆❖◆❖

Overlooked amid kabab and curry feasts, aloo gosht was the meat and potato staple of our childhood. It is only when we glance back across many winters abroad that we savor and return its loyal devotion.

The gosht meat can be mutton or chicken or beef, cooked on-the-bone or boneless, but extra credit is given for aloo gosht made with bone-in mutton.

Braise meat with onions, spices, tomatoes, and generously proportioned potatoes. Simmer until the sauce reaches the elusive consistency of a perfect saalan: no longer broth-thin nor yet sauce-thick.

Done right, aloo gosht has a confident, unvarnished richness that its flashier curry cousins envy. Its light consistency is perfect for basmati rice, so give roti and naan a miss and enjoy mouthfuls of pliant potato and succulent meat atop sauce-drenched rice.

In its nourishing simplicity and tender textures our vagrant hearts retaste our first summers. And so we beat on, migrant boats against the current, borne back ceaselessly into our aloo gosht past.*

*In homage to F. Scott Fitzgerald, *The Great Gatsby*, and one of the great endings in literature.

ALOO GOSHT
Beef and Potato Curry

½ cup ghee or oil

1 medium onion, thinly sliced

⅓ cup yogurt

3 tablespoons tomato paste

1 tablespoon ginger paste

1 tablespoon garlic paste

1 tablespoon ground coriander

1 teaspoon Garam Masala (page 215)

1 teaspoon cayenne red chili powder

1 tablespoon salt

½ teaspoon turmeric

1½ pounds boneless beef shank, cut into 1½-inch cubes

2 large potatoes, each cut in 4 pieces, 8 pieces total

½ cup chopped fresh cilantro, plus 2 tablespoons for optional garnish

2 serrano chilies

Aloo gosht, the ever-present meat curry among Pakistani households, earns its omnipresence by giving a high return in terms of nourishment and taste on relatively low investment of cooking effort. Best enjoyed with Kachumar (page 208) and Matar Pulao (page 172); otherwise Plain White Basmati Rice (page 168) will do just fine.

Traditionally made with beef or mutton, aloo gosht also works with lamb or chicken. In the recipe, you can substitute the beef with two pounds of boneless lamb or chicken thighs or use three pounds of bone-in chicken pieces. Chicken and lamb will need less time and less water to cook through.

▼▼▼▼▼▼▼▼▼▼▼▼▼▼▼▼▼▼▼▼▼▼▼▼▼▼▼▼

- In a Dutch oven, heat oil to medium heat and fry the onion slices until golden brown, about 5 to 7 minutes. Remove the onion with a slotted spoon and drain on a paper towel.

- In a blender, combine the fried onions and yogurt and blend until smooth. Set aside.

- Add the ginger and garlic to the oil in the Dutch oven and fry on medium heat for 1 to 2 minutes, until fragrant.

- Add all the spices, tomato paste, and the beef and fry for 2 to 3 minutes, stirring frequently.

- Add the onion-yogurt mixture. On low-medium heat, cook for 10 to 12 minutes, stirring occasionally, until the oil separates (the bhunnai process, see page 49).

- Add 3 cups of water, cover, and cook on medium low until meat is tender, 45 to 60 minutes, and sauce thickens to a light gravy consistency.

- When the meat is tender, add in the potatoes, cover, and cook until the potatoes are just done and a fork goes in smoothly through the potato, 10 to 12 minutes.

- Add the cilantro and chilies, lower the heat, and simmer for a few minutes. Cover and turn off the heat. Garnish with additional cilantro and serve hot.

ALOO QEEMA
Spicy Ground Beef with Potatoes

1 large onion, thinly sliced

½ cup oil

2 teaspoons ginger paste

2 teaspoons garlic paste

2 teaspoons cumin seeds

2 teaspoons ground coriander

2 teaspoons salt
(or to taste)

1 teaspoon coriander seeds,
crushed using mortar and
pestle (page 47, optional)

1½ teaspoon cayenne red
chili powder

½ teaspoon turmeric

4 medium tomatoes,
chopped

1 pound 85-percent lean
ground beef

1 large potato, diced into
1-inch cubes

¼ cup finely chopped green
onions

1 teaspoon Garam Masala
(page 215)

1 tablespoon dried fenu-
greek leaves (optional)

2 serrano chilies, thinly
sliced (optional)

¼ cup chopped fresh
cilantro

Qeema is spicy, ground meat stew; the beef can be substituted with ground chicken or lamb. The cooking time could
be reduced slightly for chicken or lamb. Potatoes are a favorite
addition, but other vegetables can be substituted (see variations). A regular star at lunch or dinner, aloo qeema also
headlines our favorite breakfast: Anda Paratha Qeema (page
88). It may be served with Plain White Basmati Rice (page 168),
Roti (page 181), or Naan (page 193), with a side of Kachumar
(page 208).

▼▼▼▼▼▼▼▼▼▼▼▼▼▼▼▼▼▼▼▼▼▼▼▼▼▼▼▼

- In a Dutch oven, fry the onion in oil over medium heat until
  golden brown, about 8 to 10 minutes.

- Add the ginger and garlic. Stir-fry for a minute.

- Add the cumin seeds, coriander, salt, crushed coriander seeds,
  cayenne, and turmeric, and fry for 1 to 2 minutes.

- Add the tomatoes and cook for 3 to 5 minutes, stirring frequently.

- Add in the ground beef and cook on medium low until the juice
  from the tomatoes is mostly absorbed.

- Add in the potato, green onions, and ½ cup water, and cook on
  low-medium heat, stirring occasionally, for 8 to 12 minutes or until
  the oil separates (the bhunna process, see page 49). The potatoes should be fork tender, the water should be dried up, and the
  oil should be seen shimmering on top.

- Sprinkle in the garam masala and fenugreek leaves. Cover and
  simmer for 5 minutes. Garnish with the chilies and cilantro.

PRO TIP

You can replace the
potatoes with other root
vegetables such as carrots
and sweet potatoes, diced
in 1-inch pieces and added
at the same point in the
recipe as the potato.

VARIATIONS

PEA (MUTTAR) QEEMA: Replace the potato with 1 to 2 cups of thawed
green peas. Add the peas once the meat is fully cooked and the oil
has risen to the top, and cook on low heat for 3 to 4 minutes before
garnishing and serving.

BELL PEPPER (SHIMLA MIRCH) QEEMA: Replace the potato with
2 medium bell peppers, cut into 1-inch square pieces. Add the bell
peppers once the meat is fully cooked and the oil has risen to the top,
and cook on low heat for 4 to 5 minutes before garnishing and serving.

EGG (ANDA) QEEMA: Go high protein and lo carb! Replace potatoes
with three hard boiled eggs cut in half, added when the meat is cooked
(no further water for cooking is needed).

KOFTA SAALAN
Spicy Meatball Curry

Succulent, spicy meatballs in a rich, flavorful sauce? Where do we sign up? Our meat of choice here is beef, but ground chicken or lamb will do just as well. Kofta saalan is delicious when enjoyed with plain rice, though a vegetarian pulao like matar pulao is a common tableside companion. As the sauce is rich and thick, rotis and naans also work well to sop it up.

▼▼▼▼▼▼▼▼▼▼▼▼▼▼▼▼▼▼▼▼▼▼▼▼▼▼

For the meatballs:

1 pound 85-percent lean ground beef

2 teaspoons ginger paste

2 teaspoons garlic paste

2 teaspoons salt

1 teaspoon cayenne red chili powder

1 teaspoon Garam Masala (page 215)

2 slices white bread

For the sauce:

1 medium onion, thinly sliced

⅓ cup oil

⅓ cup yogurt

1½ tablespoons tomato paste

1 tablespoon ground coriander

1 teaspoon ginger paste

1 teaspoon garlic paste

1 teaspoon cayenne red chili powder

½ teaspoon turmeric

1 teaspoon Garam Masala (page 215)

PRO TIP

After mixing the meat, do a taste test by pan-frying a mini meatball. Adjust the spices per your taste before shaping the rest of the meatballs.

MAKE THE MEATBALLS:

- In a large bowl, add all the meatball ingredients except the bread.

- Soak the bread slices in a bowl of water to soften. Squeeze the water out by hand and crumble the bread onto the meatball ingredients.

- Now mix all the meatball ingredients thoroughly together by hand or in a food processor.

- Take small portions of the seasoned meat (1.5 to 2 ounces) and shape into 2-inch balls (about the size of golf balls). Set aside. Note: wetting your hands or greasing them with oil can make the meatball shaping process easier.

MAKE THE SAUCE:

- In a Dutch oven, fry the onion in the oil over medium heat until golden brown, about 5 to 6 minutes. Take out the onion and leave the oil in the Dutch oven for later use.

- In a blender, add all the sauce ingredients including the fried onions, but not the oil, and blend until smooth. Add 3 tablespoons of water, if needed, to blend the ingredients together into a smooth paste.

- In the same Dutch oven used to fry the onion and using the same oil, add in the blended mixture and cook on low-medium heat, stirring frequently, for 8 to 10 minutes until the oil separates (the bhunna process, see page 49).

- Now add in 3 cups of water, increase the heat, and bring to a boil.

- Once the sauce is boiling, reduce the heat to medium and carefully slide in the meatballs with a help of a spoon.

- Cover and cook on medium low for 10 to 15 minutes until the meatballs are cooked through. Stir gently, as needed, taking care not to break the meatballs.

- Reduce the heat to a simmer and cook on low until the sauce is of desired consistency.

ON GOLA KABAB

A Karachi kabab crawl that skips the famed Shaikh Abdul Ghaffar and Waheed Kabab Houses is like a greatest cricketers compilation where Bradman and Sobers do not make the cut. The kabab that is responsible for the devoted following of both of these kabab houses is the beef gola kabab.

"Melt in your mouth" is a phrase usually reserved for delicate confections. When applied to meat entrees, the food rarely justifies such praise. Beef gola is the exception where the phrase hardly does justice to the kabab.

Having spent a night in the tenderizing embrace of raw papaya and robust spices, the marinated beef is so soft it has to be secured to skewers with threads. Hence the nickname dhaaga thread kabab for the gola kabab at Waheed's. These skewers are placed over open charcoal pits, smoked and flame-grilled to perfection, slid onto the kabab house's signature metal plates, and rushed to your table alongside wickedly hot chutney and gossamer onion strands.

The pressing question as you stare at these steaming, char-infused kababs is: Should you enjoy them with naan or sheermal saffron milk bread or paratha? The answer, of course, is D: all of the above.

GOLA KABAB
Tender Smoky Mince Patties

For the spice mix:
⅓ cup oil
1 medium onion, finely
  chopped
1 teaspoon coriander seeds
1 teaspoon cumin seeds
1 teaspoon sesame seeds
  (optional)
1 teaspoon desiccated
  coconut
1 slice white bread
2 green chili peppers,
  chopped (optional)

For the kababs:
1 pound 80-percent lean
  ground beef
2 tablespoons Greek yogurt
3 tablespoons mashed
  fresh papaya
2 teaspoons ginger paste
2 teaspoons garlic paste
1 teaspoon cayenne red
  chili powder
1 teaspoon Garam Masala
  (page 215)
1½ teaspoons salt

Raitas (page 201), for serving
Hari Chutney (page 205),
  for serving
Imli Chutney (page 206),
  for serving
Lime, sliced red onion,
  or cilantro for garnish
  (optional)

A Karachi delicacy, this kabab is so tender it is traditionally secured to skewers with threads before charcoal grilling. Note that in our recipe no threads are required nor even a charcoal grill! Feel free to substitute ground lamb for the beef.

Best enjoyed with Puri (page 197), Paratha (page 184), or Naan (page 193), but never with rice. Hari Chutney (page 205), Imli Chutney (page 206), Raitas (page 201), and Kachumar (page 208) are the favored sidekicks.

▼▼▼▼▼▼▼▼▼▼▼▼▼▼▼▼▼▼▼▼▼▼▼▼▼▼

Make the spice mix:

• In a small frying pan, heat the oil over medium heat and fry the onion until golden, about 8 minutes. Set aside.

• In a wide skillet or tava, roast the seeds and coconut over low heat for 5 to 6 minutes. Stir occasionally until the spices become fragrant. Be very careful as they burn easily.

• Use a coffee grinder to finely grind these aromatic whole spices with the bread slices, chilies, and fried onion. If your grinder cannot handle this amount of material or you do not have one, use a mortar and pestle to grind the spices, then process the spice mix ingredients in a food processor. Set aside.

MAKE THE KABABS:

• In a large bowl, mix the ground beef with the yogurt, papaya, ginger, garlic, cayenne, garam masala, salt, and prepared spice mix.

• Place the spiced beef mixture in the fridge for 3 to 4 hours, preferably overnight, to marinate and for the raw papaya enzymes to tenderize the meat.

• Using your hands, shape the marinated beef into 4-by-2.5-inch oval croquettes.

For smoking the kababs:
Aluminum foil
1 charcoal briquette
½ teaspoon oil

COOK THE KABABS:

- Either shallow-fry the kababs in a skillet over medium heat for 4 to 5 minutes on each side until golden brown; or broil the kababs on high in the oven on the middle rack for 8 to 10 minutes until golden brown.

- Transfer the kababs to a shallow casserole with a tight-fitting lid.

SMOKE THE KABABS:

- Just before serving, place a small piece of aluminum foil in the middle of the kababs, near the center of the casserole.

- Heat the charcoal briquette by using metal tongs to hold it over the open flame of a gas stove burner until it is red hot.

- Put the piece of red-hot charcoal on the aluminum foil.

- Pour the oil on the charcoal and immediately put the lid back on the casserole to contain the smoke.

- Leave for 6 to 8 minutes, allowing the kababs to become infused with charcoal smoke.

- Serve the kababs with hot naan bread, raitas, and hari and imli chutneys.

CHAPLI KABAB

Fried Spiced Patties

For the marinated meat:
1 tablespoon garlic paste
1 tablespoon red pepper
  flakes
1 tablespoon crushed
  coriander seeds
1 teaspoon dried
  pomegranate powder
  or Sumac powder
1 teaspoon coarsely
  ground black pepper
1 teaspoon salt
1 pound 80-percent lean
  ground beef
1 bunch green onion,
  6 to 8 bulbs, both green
  and white parts, finely
  chopped
1 medium tomato, finely
  diced
2 green chilies, finely
  chopped
1 tablespoon unsalted
  butter, softened
¼ cup all-purpose flour
  or chickpea flour
2 eggs, beaten

Oil, for frying
Lemon or sliced red onion
  for garnish (optional)
Bread or rice, for serving
Hara (Green) Raita (page
  203), for serving
Kachumar (page 208),
  for serving
Hari Chutney (page 205),
  for serving

Pakistan's spicier, juicier, herbier answer to hamburger patties, chapli kababs are often served as a main dish alongside Naan (page 193), Paratha (page 184), or Pulao (page 172), but they also make desirable centerpieces in sandwiches and burgers, and, for the keto lifestyle followers, garden salads. These kababs have a deliciously crispy outer crust thanks to the addition of eggs and flour. Chapli kababs are typically made with ground beef or lamb. Ground chicken, while not the traditional meat of choice, can also be used.

▼▼▼▼▼▼▼▼▼▼▼▼▼▼▼▼▼▼▼▼▼▼▼▼▼▼▼▼▼

PRO TIPS

You can use a mortar and pestle or food processor to crush the pomegranate and coriander seeds.

We recommend that you use 80-percent lean ground beef, not extra lean meat.

Dried pomegranate powder is ideal, but if not readily available substitute Sumac powder.

MAKE THE MARINATED MEAT:

• In a wide bowl, thoroughly mix the garlic paste, red pepper, coriander seeds, pomegranate seeds, black pepper, and salt with the ground beef.

• Add the green onion, tomato, chilies, butter, flour, and beaten eggs, and mix thoroughly for several minutes, using your hand to combine all marinade ingredients evenly into the ground beef.

• Marinate for at least 1 hour in the fridge.

• Using your hands, form medium balls of 3-to-5-ounce portions, and then flatten them into oval-shaped patties. The edges and middle of the patty should be the same thickness, about ⅓ inch.

• Heat a small amount of oil over medium heat in a skillet.

• Shallow-fry the patties in the oil for about 5 minutes on each side, pressing with a spatula to ensure the kababs are crispy and golden brown on both sides. Only flip once; avoid the temptation to turn them over several times.

• Serve hot with your choice of bread or rice, accompanied by green raita, kachumar, and hari chutney.

MEMONI CRISPY FRIED LAMB CHOPS
WITH MASHED POTATO CRUST

For the marinade:
6 Thai green chilies
1 cup coarsely chopped
   fresh cilantro with stems
½ cup coarsely chopped
   fresh mint leaves
½ cup water
1 cup plain yogurt
1 teaspoon Garam Masala
   (page 215)
1 tablespoon ginger paste
1 tablespoon garlic paste
1 teaspoon cayenne red
   chili powder
1 teaspoon salt (or to taste)
2 pounds lamb chops,
   excess fat well-trimmed

For the mashed potato crust:
2 large potatoes, peeled and
   cut into 2-inch cubes
5 to 6 cups water
1 teaspoon salt (or to taste)
½ teaspoon freshly ground
   black pepper
½ teaspoon red pepper
   flakes (optional)

For frying and serving:
2 eggs
1 teaspoon cornstarch
1 tablespoon water
2 cups panko or regular
   bread crumbs
Oil, for deep-frying
¼ teaspoon Chaat Masala
   (page 214), optional
Hari Chutney (page 205),
   for serving

In Pakistani home cooking, lamb or mutton chops are often marinated in spices, then gently cooked over low heat on the stovetop until all spices are completely absorbed and the meat is tender. The family recipe we follow here is a Memoni variation for crispy fried lamb chops that has been passed down many generations. Here the slow-cooked lamb chops are breaded and fried before serving. The other Memoni secret here is the "green masala" marinade which adds a spicy-herby richness to the chops.

As a special treat, my mother would sometimes coat the cooked lamb chops with mashed potatoes, then egg-crumb-fry them. We include this step in our recipe here to give an extra dimension to our lamb chops. You can skip it to reduce the effort—or if you love the result as much as we do, you can apply it to the Memoni Crispy Fried Chicken (page 95) as well.

We usually serve these with Tarka Daal (page 159) and Plain White Basmati Rice (page 168), though they can also be paired with Baked Masala Potato Wedges (page 74) and ketchup.

▼▼▼▼▼▼▼▼▼▼▼▼▼▼▼▼▼▼▼▼▼▼▼▼▼▼▼▼

PRO TIPS

Don't worry about the heat level here, the chops lose marinade and become milder when fried. I love the fragrance and flavor of Thai chilies but you can always substitute with other less potent green chilies like serrano or jalapeño.

The ready-to-fry chops freeze really well. After cooking and coating, line them on a baking sheet and put in freezer for a few hours. When frozen-hard, pack them in a freezer bag and store. When ready to use, defrost and fry.

Want to forgo the frying? Spray the panko-coated pieces with olive oil and place on a nonstick oiled baking sheet. Bake at 400 degrees F for about 20 minutes until golden crispy.

MARINATE AND COOK LAMB CHOPS:

- In a blender, add green chilies, cilantro, mint, and water, and blend to make a hara green masala paste.

- In a medium bowl, mix green masala paste, yogurt, garam masala, ginger, garlic, cayenne, and salt, using a fork, to make the marinade.

- Add the chops and marinate overnight or for at least 4 hours.
- In a Dutch oven, cook the marinated chops on low-medium heat until the chops are fully cooked and tender, about 25 to 30 minutes. Note that no oil is needed as the lamb will slow-cook in the yogurt-based marinade. If chops are still tough, you may add a little water (about ½ cup) and cook on medium low until the water dries and masala is clinging to the chops. Chops should be tender but not be falling off the bone.

MAKE THE MASHED POTATO CRUST:

- In a medium saucepan, bring about 5 cups of water, enough to cover the potatoes, to boil.
- Add potatoes and boil for 12 to 15 minutes or until fork tender.
- Drain water and mash potatoes using a potato masher or large fork.
- Add salt, pepper, and red pepper flakes. Mix well and set aside.

CRUST AND FRY THE LAMB CHOPS:

- In a shallow bowl, beat the eggs with cornstarch and water.
- Put the bread crumbs in a platter.
- Use your hands to press about a tablespoon of mashed potato onto both sides of each lamb chop.
- Now dip the chops, one at a time, first in the egg mixture and then in the bread crumbs.
- Heat 2 inches of oil in a wok or karahi to 325 degrees F. Test that oil is ready for deep-frying using the wooden spoon test (see Desi Pantry, page 32). Deep-fry lamb chops on medium high until the lamb chops are golden, about 2 minutes on both sides.
- Remove and place chops on a paper towel.
- Sprinkle lightly with chaat masala and accompany with hari chutney.

ON NIHARI

＊◆＊

There are many contenders for the world's second-best stew.
For anyone who has experienced it, the top spot forever belongs
to nihari.

Born in Delhi in the dying days of the Mughal dynasty, nihari was
brought to Pakistan by refugees from that famed city. The great
legacy of the Delhiwallas in Karachi remains the Burns Road nihari.

Burns Road is the culinary heart of Karachi. Twenty million
citizens course through congested arteries to get their cheap
feasts here. Walk past smoky stalls and blaring humanity to enter
any of its famed nihari houses. Stark, airy, garishly lit, their interi-
ors make no concessions to suburban sensibilities and comforts.
Their white-surfaced tables and sturdy wooden chairs are clean
canvases for the great works of art served up daily.

As you survey the laden tables of your fellow patrons, the
efficient servers will bring out your nihari and naans. The thick,
shimmering beef stew in front of you—its surface glistening with
cayenne-red oil, flecked with ginger strands and green chilies—
was prepared all night and all day for you. Large chunks of shank
meat and marrow bones were simmered overnight in a harem of
spices, made velvety with a flour roux in the morning, and kept
smoldering through the afternoon.

With a burly piece of naan, pull apart the tender meat and quench
it in the hot stew. As you indulge, consider every possible analogy,
nominee, recollection, and label for great stew—and fall short.

You may, with complete disregard for moderation, opt for the
buttery, saffron sweetness of sheermal instead of naan. Pro tip:
order both. Having seen such wanton behavior daily, your servers
will replenish your naans and sheermals and nihari plates without
passing judgment on your perspiring gluttony. Tip them well.

This gastronomy/aromatherapy/sauna package will set you
back about $3 and you shall repent the Michelin excesses and
eco-spa detoxes of your misspent past.

Eating nihari at Burns Road is a sweltering, voracious, primal
phenomenon—like Karachi itself.

NIHARI

Pakistani Beef Stew

For the flour slurry:
½ cup all-purpose flour
2 cups water

For the nihari masala spices:
1 tablespoon fennel seeds
1 tablespoon dried ginger
   powder
1 tablespoon corainder
   seeds
1 piece mace
¼ piece nutmeg
5 white cardamom pods
1 black cardamom pod
8 to 10 black peppercorns
1 teaspoon Garam Masala
   (pg 215)

⅓ cup oil
1 medium onion, sliced
2 pound boneless beef shank,
   cut into 3-inch chunks
½ pound beef marrow bones
1 teaspoon ginger paste
1 tablespoon garlic paste
1 teaspoon ground coriander
1½ teaspoons cayenne red
   chili powder
2 teaspoons paprika or
   Kashmiri red chili powder
1½ teaspoons salt
½ teaspoon ground turmeric
Lemons, sliced, for serving,
Green chilies, finely sliced,
   for serving
Ginger, julienned, for serving

For the tarka (optional):
1 small onion, thinly sliced
¼ cup ghee or oil
2 tablespoon white vinegar
½ teaspoon paprika

According to most of us, nihari is Pakistan's national dish.

Making nihari for loved ones is a labor of love. In our recipe we try to make the traditional a bit more accessible without cutting any corners on authentic taste and texture. While lamb and chicken variants exist, beef is the preferred meat for nihari. Our recipe can be adapted to lamb and chicken by substituting the beef and skipping the beef marrow. Nihari is one of the very few curries that is best enjoyed with piping hot naan and not with rice.

▼▼▼▼▼▼▼▼▼▼▼▼▼▼▼▼▼▼▼▼▼▼▼▼▼▼▼▼▼

MAKE FLOUR SLURRY:

• In a bowl, add all-purpose flour to water. Whisk and set aside.

MAKE NIHARI MASALA:

• Using a coffee grinder, grind all the nihari masala spices finely.

• Sieve through a fine sifter to get rid of any large pieces.

• In a medium bowl, add ground spices and ½ cup water, mixing to make a masala paste. Set aside.

PREPARE THE NIHARI MEAT:

• In a large heavy-bottomed pot, heat ½ cup oil, add in sliced onions, and cook on medium heat until onion slices turn golden, 5 to 6 minutes.

• Add in the beef shank, marrow bones, ginger, garlic, coriander, cayenne red chili powder, paprika, salt, turmeric, and the nihari masala paste. Cook for 6 to 8 minutes on medium heat.

• Add in about 8 cups of water and bring to a boil.

• Once the nihari sauce starts to boil, turn the heat down to low, and cover the pot tightly with a large piece of foil followed by a tight-fitting lid.

• Cook for 1 to 1½ hour or until meat is fork tender.

PREPARE THE NIHARI CURRY:

- Turn off heat. Gently remove the meat to a casserole dish and set aside. Discard the bones.

- Using a large spoon, skim off the red chili oil that should have come to the top. Set aside for later use.

- Turn heat back on and increase to medium high. Now slowly add in the flour slurry, stirring constantly.

- Keep stirring until the sauce comes to a boil.

- Reduce heat to simmer and cook for 30 minutes, stirring occasionally as the flour can burn easily.

- Adjust the consistency of the sauce by either adding more water or more flour slurry, as needed. Sauce should have the consistency of a rich bisque.

- With heat still at simmer, slide the meat back into the curry, add the red chili oil and turn off the stove.

- *Make the tarka:* Heat ghee or oil on medium and fry onions for 5 to 6 minutes until golden brown. Turn off heat. Now stir in the vinegar and paprika to add color to oil.

- Add tarka to the pot and cover until ready to serve.

- Garnish with finely sliced green chilies and julienned ginger, and serve with lemon wedges on the side.

v.

MACHLI

❖•••••••••••••••••••••••❖

From the
Arabian Sea

MASALA FISH FRY

For the marinade:
½ teaspoon garlic paste
½ teaspoon ground turmeric
¼ teaspoon cayenne red
  chili powder
½ teaspoon red pepper
  flakes
1 tablespoon crushed
  coriander seeds
2 tablespoons freshly
  squeezed lime or
  lemon juice
¼ teaspoon crushed
  carom seeds
1 teaspoon salt

1 pound fish fillets (any
  firm fish, such as halibut,
  salmon, or sea bass)
¼ cup all-purpose flour or
  gram flour (besan)
½ cup oil
¼ teaspoon Chaat Masala
  (page 214)
Lemon wedges, for garnish

You knew the Pakistani take on fried fish would be complex-flavored and pack an almighty punch. But thankfully the preparation and frying remain far from complex.

Serve this dish as the star of any lunch or dinner. Best enjoyed in the company of a "wet" dish such as Tarka Daal (page 159) and an aromatic rice—we recommend Matar Pulao (page 172).

▼▼▼▼▼▼▼▼▼▼▼▼▼▼▼▼▼▼▼▼▼▼▼▼▼▼

MAKE THE MARINADE:

- In a small bowl, mix all the marinade ingredients.
- Clean fish fillets with water and pat dry with paper towel.
- Smear the marinade over fish filets and let the fish marinate for at least 15 minutes or overnight in the fridge. If frying later, refrigerate marinated fish until you are ready to cook.
- Put the flour in a wide, shallow plate.
- In large frying pan, heat the oil to medium heat.
- Gently dab the fish filets one at a time in flour to lightly coat both sides.
- Fry the fish filets in oil, 2 to 3 minutes on each side or until fully cooked.
- Drain the fish on a paper towel. Sprinkle with chaat masala and serve with lemon wedges.

FISH SHAMI KABABS
Desi Tuna Croquettes

For the daal mixture:
1 cup split Bengal gram (chana daal)
2½ cups water
½ medium onion
1 tablespoon finely chopped ginger
5 garlic cloves
1 tablespoon red pepper flakes
1 teaspoon cumin seeds
1 teaspoon salt (or to taste)

½ cup panko bread crumbs
1 teaspoon Garam Masala (page 215)
1 (12-ounce) can tuna, in water
1 large egg
½ cup chopped onion
¼ cup chopped fresh cilantro
¼ cup chopped fresh mint
1 green chili pepper, finely chopped (optional)
Oil, for frying
Hari Chutney (page 205), for serving

PRO TIP

You can freeze unfried fish cake patties until needed. This is best done by freezing the patties on a greased or parchment-lined baking sheet, then transferring to a freezer bag when frozen through. Defrost patties to room temperature before frying.

These fish cakes are made from a tuna, lentil, and herb mix, formed into patties, and pan fried. They are equally at home in a school lunchbox, at a weekend soiree, for a quick mid-week dinner, or on a coastal picnic. For a light and flavorful lunch, pair with a vegetarian or lentil dish and serve alongside Plain White Basmati Rice (page 168).

▼▼▼▼▼▼▼▼▼▼▼▼▼▼▼▼▼▼▼▼▼▼▼▼▼▼

- In a medium bowl of water, soak the lentils; there should be enough water to cover the lentils completely. Set aside for a few hours, preferably overnight. Drain before using.

- In a medium saucepan, add the soaked lentils, 2½ cups water, the onion, ginger, garlic, red pepper flakes, and cumin. Do not add the salt at this point, as it will keep the lentils from cooking properly. Cook over medium heat at a gentle boil for 30 minutes or until the lentils are tender but not mushy. Add a little more water if the lentils are still hard in the center. Cook until the water has evaporated and lentil mixture is quite dry, not runny, before turning off the stove.

- Transfer lentil mixture to a food processor, add in the salt, and grind until smooth.

- Pour the mixture into a pan and let it cool down completely.

- Add the bread crumbs and garam masala to the lentil mixture and mix well.

- Squeeze out all the water from the tuna and add it to the lentil mixture, mixing well. Add in the egg, onion, cilantro, mint, and chili, and mix well.

- Using your hands, form into 3-inch-diameter patties.

- In a medium frying pan, heat the oil and shallow-fry the patties for 1 to 2 minutes on each side until crispy and golden brown.

- Serve with hari chutney.

MEMONI COCONUT SHRIMP CURRY

Green Masala Shrimps in Coconut Milk

1 pound raw shrimp

⅓ cup oil, plus 2 tablespoons

¼ cup chopped cilantro

5 Thai green chilies

2 teaspoons garlic paste

2 teaspoons ginger paste

½ teaspoon turmeric powder

1 teaspoon Garam Masala (page 215)

1 teaspoon cayenne chili powder

1½ teaspoons salt (or to taste)

⅓ teaspoon mustard seeds

1 small onion, thinly sliced

2 tablespoons desiccated coconut

½ cup coconut milk

1 tablespoon lemon juice

PRO TIP

For best results, use raw shrimp in this recipe. You can use precooked shrimps if you wish: just stir them in toward the end. It is important not to overcook shrimps as extended cooking will make them tough and chewy.

There is shrimp curry, and then there is shrimp curry made by a Memon mom. Luckily, I grew up savoring the latter. Coconut Shrimp Curry was a perennial favorite at our home. The secret lies in pairing a piquant green masala paste with rich coconut milk. It is best enjoyed atop that great canvas for all works of desi culinary art, Plain White Basmati Rice (page 168).

▼▼▼▼▼▼▼▼▼▼▼▼▼▼▼▼▼▼▼▼▼▼▼▼▼▼▼

- Devein, wash, and drain the shrimp in a colander.

- Heat 2 tablespoon of oil in a pan and flash-fry the shrimps on medium high. As soon as they turn salmon-pink, take them out and set aside.

- Make green masala paste: Blend chopped cilantro, Thai chillies, and ¼ cup water in a blender and set aside.

- Make ginger-garlic paste: In a bowl, combine ginger, garlic, turmeric, garam masala, cayenne chili powder, and salt with 2 tablespoons of water and set aside.

- In a wok bring ⅓ cup of oil to medium heat. Add mustard seeds followed by onion, and fry until golden, about 7 to 8 minutes. Add dessicated coconut and stir-fry for a minute or so. Stir in the ginger-garlic paste and fry for a few minutes until the oil separates.

- Now add the green masala paste and coconut milk, and stir for a minute. Finally, stir in the shrimps and lemon juice, cover wok, and turn off heat.

- Serve with Plain Basmati Rice (page 168) and Kachumar (page 208).

LAAL MASALA FISH

Fish in Spicy Tomato Sauce

2 small to medium fillets
   of any firm fish, such as
   halibut, bass, salmon, cod,
   or tilapia.
¼ cup plus ½ cup oil, divided
1 tablespoon red pepper
   flakes (or to taste)
2 cups tomato puree
½ teaspoon salt (or to taste)
½ bunch cilantro, finely
   chopped (about ½ cup)

This exotic dish will dazzle your guests' palates, yet it can be made in about fifteen minutes: fried fish topped with unique tomato ragout, garnished with fresh cilantro. The sauce for this dish is similar to that used in Baked Masala Potatoes Wedges (page 74).

▾▾▾▾▾▾▾▾▾▾▾▾▾▾▾▾▾▾▾▾▾▾▾▾▾▾

- Clean fish fillets with water and pat dry with paper towel. Set aside.

- In a large frying pan, heat ¼ cup oil on medium heat and sear the fish for about 1 minute on each side until golden and until almost done. Remove and set aside.

- In a medium saucepan, heat remaining ½ cup oil on medium heat, add crushed pepper and just as they start to sizzle, quickly add the tomato puree and salt.

- Fry the tomato/chili paste on medium low until it has the consistency of a thick sauce and oil separates out on top, about 6 to 8 minutes.

- Gently slide fried fish into the pan.

- Simmer for 3 to 5 minutes or until fish is fully done and flakes easily.

- Garnish with cilantro and serve.

VI

SABZI

···•···•···•···•···•···•···•···

Vegetarian
Delights

TURAI SABZI ⓥ

Zucchini Stew

¼ cup ghee or oil

2 cups chopped onion

2 Roma tomatoes, chopped

½ teaspoon cayenne red
  chili powder (optional)

¼ teaspoon ground turmeric

1 teaspoon cumin seeds

½ teaspoon salt (or to taste)

4 medium zucchinis, peeled
  and sliced

The sweetness of zucchini and onion balances the relatively mild ensemble of spices in this simple vegetarian stew. The absence of garlic, ginger, and many of the other staples of subcontinental stews lets the zucchini take center stage. It is frequently cast at lunch and dinner alongside a lentil and a meat main, and a steaming platter of Plain White Basmati Rice (page 168).

- In a medium saucepan, heat the ghee on medium heat and sauté the onion until translucent, about 1 minute—do not brown. This will keep them sweet to taste.

- Add in the tomatoes and all the spices. Cook on medium-low heat, stirring frequently, for 10 to 12 minutes, until the oil rises (the bhunna process, see page 49).

- Add in the zucchini and mix well. Cover and cook on low, stirring occasionally, until the zucchini is tender, 12 to 15 minutes. There is no need to add water as the moisture of the zucchini, tomatoes, and onion should be enough.

PALAK

Palak or palag means spinach in Urdu, and Pakistanis enjoy many vegetarian and nonvegetarian spinach-based stews. We include here two of the most popular spinach stews, one featuring potatoes (aloo palak) and another featuring a firm cottage cheese (palak paneer).

ALOO PALAK (v)
Spinach Stew with Potatoes

½ cup ghee or oil

1 large onion, thinly sliced

1 teaspoon ginger paste

1 teaspoon garlic paste

½ teaspoon cayenne red chili powder

1½ teaspoons salt (or to taste)

¼ teaspoon ground turmeric

1½ teaspoons cumin seeds

1 teaspoon ground coriander

1 (16-ounce) package frozen chopped spinach, or 1½ pounds fresh spinach leaves

¾ cup milk

1 large potato, peeled and cut into 1-inch cubes

2 whole serrano chilies (optional)

1 teaspoon Garam Masala (page 215)

1½ tablespoons dried fenugreek leaves

2 tablespoons of unsalted butter (optional)

¼ cup chopped fresh cilantro

This is a vegetarian main dish, and when placed alongside a well-made lentil stew and rice, it needs no meaty interventions. Nevertheless, in Pakistan, a meat curry and roti or paratha are often added to the menu.

* In a medium saucepan, heat the ghee on medium heat.
* Add the onion to the oil and fry for 10 minutes until lightly golden.
* Add in the ginger and garlic and stir-fry for 1 minute.
* Add the cayenne, salt, turmeric, cumin seeds, and coriander and cook for 1 minute.
* Add the spinach and milk, stir well, and cook covered on medium-low heat for about 20 minutes.
* Add the potato cubes, chilies, garam masala, and fenugreek leaves, and cover. Cook on low heat until potatoes are cooked through, about 8 to 10 minutes. Now cook uncovered on medium heat, stirring occasionally, until most of the moisture is gone and the potatoes are fork tender.
* Place in a serving dish, add the butter, and stir. Garnish with cilantro. Serve hot.

PALAK PANEER ⓥ
Spinach Stew with Cottage Cheese

½ cup ghee or oil

1 large onion, thinly sliced

1 teaspoon ginger paste

1 teaspoon garlic paste

½ teaspoon cayenne red chili powder

1½ teaspoons salt (or to taste)

¼ teaspoon ground turmeric

1½ teaspoons cumin seeds

1 teaspoon ground coriander

1 (16-ounce) package frozen chopped spinach, or 1½ pounds fresh spinach leaves

¾ cup milk

1 (8-ounce) package of paneer, cut into 1-inch cubes

2 whole serrano chilies (optional)

1 teaspoon Garam Masala (page 215)

1½ tablespoons dried fenugreek leaves

2 tablespoons of unsalted butter (optional)

¼ cup chopped fresh cilantro

Paneer, a firm cottage cheese, is a staple of Indian vegetarian cuisine. Less popular in Pakistan, it is now increasingly seen on Pakistani dinner tables at home and on those of the Pakistani diaspora abroad. Like aloo palak, this serves as a vegetarian main dish or a companion to a meat dish on equal footing.

▼▼▼▼▼▼▼▼▼▼▼▼▼▼▼▼▼▼▼▼▼▼▼▼▼▼▼

PRO TIPS

To get a nice color to the paneer cubes, you can stir-fry them in oil or ghee separately on medium heat, for 3 to 5 minutes, until light golden brown. Remove and keep aside until ready to add to the stewed spinach.

Avoiding dairy? Substitute coconut milk for regular milk and tofu for paneer and add at the same time as the paneer, and use oil instead of ghee.

- Follow the Aloo Palak recipe (page 147), but substitute the paneer for the potato.

- Add the paneer cubes when you would add the potatoes. Cover and cook on low heat for about 8 minutes. Now cook uncovered on medium heat, stirring occasionally, until most of the moisture is gone.

- Place in a serving dish, add the butter and stir. Garnish with cilantro. Serve hot.

ALOO TIKKI Ⓥ
Crispy Mashed Potato Cutlets

For the mashed potatoes:
4 medium potatoes (about 1½ pounds), peeled
1 tablespoon ghee or oil

For the dry spices:
½ teaspoon cayenne red chili powder
1 teaspoon red pepper flakes
2 garlic cloves, crushed
½ teaspoon cumin seeds
1 teaspoon crushed coriander seeds
½ teaspoon ground turmeric
⅛ teaspoon carom seeds (ajwain)

1 tablespoon chopped fresh mint leaves
1 serrano chili, finely diced, deseed if desired (optional)
1 teaspoon salt
½ cup bread crumbs
¼ cup oil
Raita (page 201), Garlic-Chili Ketchup (page 207), Hari Chutney (page 205), or Imli Chutney (page 206), for serving

PRO TIPS

If possible, keep the boiled and peeled potatoes in the fridge overnight to dry completely.

If the potato cutlets are not holding their shape during frying, add more bread crumbs into the mixture.

Cornstarch or rice flour (3 to 4 tablespoons) can be substituted for the bread crumbs for a gluten-free version.

As popular as they are easy to make, aloo tikkis are crispy on the outside and succulent and spicy on the inside. Their allure may well cause vegetarian envy among traditionally meat-loving Pakistanis, especially when served in bun kababs—(page 70). Versatile aloo tikkis are served as vegetarian mains, as sides to meat dishes, as salad toppers, and as fillings in sliders, burgers, wraps, and rolls. Whatever the occasion, chutneys and kachumar are the aloo tikki's best friend.

- In a medium pot, bring about 6 cups of water to boil over high heat. Lower the heat to medium, then add the potatoes and boil for 10 to 15 minutes until just done; overboiling will make the potatoes mushy. Test doneness by inserting a toothpick or fork into the center: it should pass easily through without resistance. Drain and set aside, preferably for several hours in the fridge, until they are cool and dry.
- Mash or grate the potatoes and set aside.
- In a small saucepan, heat the oil over low heat and add all the dry spices and serrano chili, if using. Lightly fry for 2 to 3 minutes until fragrant.
- Allow the spice mixture to cool, then add to the mashed potatoes. Add in the mint, chilies, salt, and bread crumbs, and mix thoroughly.
- Using your hands, shape into ½-inch-thick round cutlets, each about 3 inches in diameter. You should have 6 to 8 cutlets.
- In a large frying pan, shallow-fry the cutlets in the oil over medium heat until golden brown, 2 to 3 minutes on each side. Be careful not to overcrowd the pan.
- Drain on a paper towel. Serve hot with raita, garlic-chili ketchup, and hari chutney or imli chutney. Garnish with chilies, sliced red onion, and cilantro.

LAAL MASALA ALOO

Fingerling Potatoes in Spicy Tomato Sauce

12 fingerling or baby
potatoes (about 1 pound)
½ cup ghee or oil
1 tablespoon red pepper
flakes
2 cups tomato puree
1 teaspoon salt (or to taste)
½ bunch cilantro, finely
chopped (about ½ cup)

In this simple dish we top whole fingerling potatoes with a spicy tomato ragout and garnish with fresh cilantro. This is a no-fuss all-flavor way to brighten up a brunch, lunch, or dinner. Its striking, red-hot looks make it the easiest of side dishes for a dinner party menu. We share a similar pescatarian recipe Laal Masala Fish (page 143).

▼▼▼▼▼▼▼▼▼▼▼▼▼▼▼▼▼▼▼▼▼▼▼▼▼▼▼

• Boil the fingerling potatoes until cooked. Test the doneness by inserting a toothpick or fork into the center: it should pass easily through without resistance.

• Take out of pot and allow to cool down. Gently peel away the skin from the potatoes with your fingers or use a butter knife.

• In a medium saucepan, heat the oil over medium heat, add the crushed pepper and just as they start to sizzle, quickly add the tomato puree and salt.

• Fry the tomato/chili paste on medium low until it has the consistency of a thick sauce and the oil separates out on top, 6 to 8 minutes.

• Reduce the heat to a simmer and add the potatoes. Stir the potatoes occasionally (and gently!) to coat them with the sauce. Cook for about 5 minutes.

• Garnish with the cilantro and serve.

ZEERA ALOO ⓥ

Cumin-Laced Potatoes

3 medium potatoes (about 1½ pounds)
¼ to ½ cup ghee or oil
1 teaspoon cumin seeds
1 tablespoon chili sauce; we like sambal chili paste, or you can use our Red Hot Garlic-Chili Chutney, (page 207)
¼ teaspoon ground turmeric
½ teaspoon salt (or to taste)
½ cup water
1 tablespoon finely chopped fresh cilantro

Zeera aloo is a quick-and-easy potato dish whose memorable flavor comes from aromatic cumin seeds sautéed alongside a selective ensemble of seasonings. As this is a "dry" dish, i.e. not a stew, it is a great dish to have beside a "wet" curry or Tarka Daal (page 159), and a satisfying filling for a vegetarian roti or Paratha (page 184). It is also one of our favorite potato sides at weekend brunches. Serve with hot Roti (page 181) or Paratha (page 184), accompanied by Kachumar (page 208) and Raitas (page 201).

▾▾▾▾▾▾▾▾▾▾▾▾▾▾▾▾▾▾▾▾▾▾▾▾▾▾

◆ Peel and slice the potatoes into thin, half-moon-shaped slices, ⅓ to ¼ inch thick. Soak in water until ready to use.

◆ In a large saucepan, heat the ghee on medium low.

◆ Add the cumin seeds, and fry for 30 seconds to release their aroma. Then add the sliced potatoes, chili sauce, turmeric, and salt. Stir gently to coat the potatoes with the cumin seeds and spices, 1 to 2 minutes.

◆ Cover and cook on low, gently turning the potatoes over occasionally, until the potatoes are done and fork tender, 6 to 8 minutes.

◆ Garnish with cilantro and serve.

BHINDI MASALA ⓥ
Spiced Okra in Tomato-Onion Sauce

1 pound fresh baby okra

½ cup ghee or oil

1 teaspoon minced garlic

2 Roma tomatoes, finely chopped

½ teaspoon red pepper flakes

¼ teaspoon ground turmeric

1 teaspoon cumin seeds

¾ teaspoon salt (or to taste)

1 medium onion, sliced

2 serrano chilies (optional)

Julienned ginger (optional)

1 tablespoon freshly squeezed lemon juice (optional)

Bhindi is a perennial favorite in Pakistani homes. In this recipe the okra is stir-fried first before being added to a delicately spiced tomato-onion sauce. It's usually accompanied by Tarka Daal (page 159) and enjoyed with Plain White Basmati Rice (page 168), Roti (page 181), or both.

▾▾▾▾▾▾▾▾▾▾▾▾▾▾▾▾▾▾▾▾▾▾▾▾▾▾▾

- Rinse the okra in water and dry with a paper towel. Cut the stalk end off the okra and discard. Cut each pod into two or three pieces about 1 inch long.

- To a medium saucepan, add 3 tablespoons of ghee and the okra, and stir-fry over medium heat for 6 to 7 minutes until the okra is a vibrant green color and glistens. Remove the pan from heat, take the okra out, and set aside.

- Wipe the pan clean with a paper towel, add the remaining ghee, and heat on medium. Add the garlic and stir-fry for 30 seconds, then add the tomatoes, red pepper flakes, turmeric, cumin seeds, and salt. Stir-fry for about 5 minutes until the tomatoes soften.

- Add in the fried okra and the onion. Turn the heat to low, cover, and cook until the okra is tender and the onion is translucent, stirring occasionally, 8 to 10 minutes.

- Garnish with the chilies and ginger and sprinkle with the lemon juice.

TARKA DAAL (Vg)
Yellow Lentils with Chile-Cumin Oil

1 cup split yellow lentils or
 split red lentils
1 teaspoon ground turmeric
¾ teaspoon salt (or to taste)
Tarka (recipe follows)

PRO TIPS

Soaking overnight will
improve the nutritional
benefits of the lentils.

Don't add salt until the
lentils are almost cooked.
Adding salt earlier in the
cooking slows down the tenderizing of the lentil grains
and increases cooking time.

Our recipe can be made
with red lentils or yellow
lentils. Try both and see
which you love best, or mix
them half and half.

For a tangy variation, stir
1 tablespoon of freshly
squeezed lime juice or 1
tablespoon of tamarind pulp
into the daal, just before
adding the tarka.

Light, simple, and flavorful, it is no wonder why daal is a
perennial favorite in South Asian homes. At our home, red
lentils are slow-cooked in a turmeric-accented broth, then
topped with a flavored oil. Daal is a truly versatile dish: serve
as a flavorful soup, a headlining vegetarian stew, or a delicious
side to a main at nearly every meal. Plain White Basmati Rice
(page 168), Roti (page 181), or Naan (page 193) are all equally
popular companions.

• In a medium bowl, rinse and soak the lentils in enough water to
  cover them, for at least 1 hour or overnight. Drain the water when
  ready to use.

• In a deep pot, add the lentils, 3 cups of water, and the turmeric.
  Do not add salt at this point.

• Bring to a rapid boil and keep over high heat for 4 to 5 minutes,
  skimming off any froth and stirring frequently.

• Turn the heat down to medium low and cook until the lentils
  are thick and saucy, and the lentil grains are soft to the touch,
  another 35 to 40 minutes. Now add the salt and stir.

• Turn the heat down to low and keep the lentils warm on the stove
  while you make the tarka.

• Quickly add the hot tarka to the lentils. Don't stir; let the tarka
  stay on top.

• Ladle the daal out into a serving bowl and serve immediately.

Tarka
Chile-Cumin Oil

¼ cup ghee or oil
4 dried red chili peppers
½ teaspoon cumin seeds
4 garlic cloves, thinly sliced
½ small onion, thinly sliced
6 fresh curry leaves
 (optional)
Cilantro (optional)

Tarka (flavored oil, also called bhagar) is made by flash-frying
cumin and dried red peppers in ghee—a process similar to
tempering, see page 42.

• Heat the ghee (or oil) in a frying pan over medium heat.

• Add the peppers, followed by the seeds, garlic, onion, and curry
  leaves. Fry until the onion and garlic turn golden brown, 3 to
  4 minutes. Garnish with cilantro.

KAALI MASOOR KI DAAL

Black Lentils with Chile-Cumin Oil

For the daal:
1 cup black lentils
¼ teaspoon ground turmeric
½ teaspoon cayenne red
   chili powder
1 teaspoon ground coriander
1 teaspoon Garam Masala
   (page 215)
2 tablespoons tomato paste
   or 2 Roma tomatoes,
   chopped
1 tablespoon tamarind pulp
2 tablespoons chopped
   fresh mint
1 ½ teaspoons salt
3 to 4 serrano chilies
1 to 2 tablespoons chopped
   fresh cilantro

Tarka (see recipe on
   page 159)

Daal dishes in Pakistan come in two varieties: wet daals, which have a curry-like or soupy consistency, and dry daals, which have little to no liquid. This recipe is our favorite dry daal. As children, we always welcomed it as a refreshing change to the yellow daal that appeared at nearly every home-cooked meal. This dish, often simply called kaali daal, or black lentils, goes well with any meat or vegetarian curry. Being a dry item, Raita (page 201) is almost a compulsory accessory. Roti (page 181) or Paratha (page 184) overtake rice as the preferred accompanying starch.

▼▼▼▼▼▼▼▼▼▼▼▼▼▼▼▼▼▼▼▼▼▼▼▼▼▼▼

- In a medium bowl, rinse and soak the lentils in enough water to cover them, for at least 1 hour or overnight. Drain the water when ready to use. Soaking lentils is optional but highly recommended.

- In a large saucepan, add the soaked lentils, 5½ cups of water, the turmeric, cayenne, coriander, garam masala, and tomato paste. Do not add salt at this point as it slows down the cooking. Bring to a boil.

- Cover and cook on medium heat, allowing the lentils to cook on a gentle boil for 45 minutes to 1 hour, stirring occasionally. Cook until the lentils are done soft to touch.

- Mash a few lentils with a spoon to get a thicker consistency.

- Add the tamarind pulp, mint, and salt, and stir.

- Cover and let simmer until the tarka is ready to pour over the cooked lentils.

- Add the tarka (page 159) over the lentils but do not stir in. Turn off the heat, and cover until ready to serve. Garnish with chilies and cilantro before serving.

ROASTED EGGPLANT YOGURT ⓥ

1 large eggplant
¼ teaspoon olive oil
½ cup Greek yogurt
¼ teaspoon salt (or to taste)
¼ teaspoon freshly ground
   black pepper
3 tablespoons extra-virgin
   olive oil
1 green onion, green and
   white parts, finely
   chopped

Lying somewhere between a fancy dip and a simple but tasty side dish, this is an ideal lunch item on the long hot Karachi summer days. In a nod to its Mediterranean composition, we replace regular yogurt with Greek yogurt in our recipe. This is a delicious companion to kababs, at home in a vegetarian meal alongside spinach and lentil entrees, or a tasty standalone snack with Naan (page 193) or Roti (page 181).

- Prick the eggplant with a fork on all sides. Smear the eggplant with the oil until well coated.

- On a medium open flame of a gas range burner, roast the eggplant on all sides until the skin is charred and the eggplant is soft and cooked through, 8 to 10 minutes. Alternatively, broil in an oven set on high for 10 to 15 minutes, rotating to broil on all sides.

- Let it cool on a rack.

- Peel off the skin. You can keep the stalk intact and discard any liquid.

- Place the eggplant on a cutting board and chop finely with a knife.

- In a medium bowl, whisk the yogurt with the salt and pepper. Add in the eggplant and mix well.

- Drizzle the olive oil on top and garnish with the green onion.

LAHORI CHOLAY

Lahore-Style Chickpea Stew

1 tablespoon ginger paste

1 tablespoon garlic paste

¼ cup mashed potato

1 teaspoon salt (or to taste)

½ teaspoon freshly ground black pepper, plus more for garnish

¼ teaspoon baking soda

1 teaspoon red pepper flakes

¼ teaspoon turmeric

¼ cup yogurt

½ cup oil

1 cup finely chopped onion

2 (15-ounce) cans chickpeas (garbanzo) with liquid

2 to 3 green chilies, sliced or whole (optional)

2 boiled eggs, peeled and sliced (optional)

2 tablespoons chopped cilantro (optional)

It takes a lot to be a favorite offering in that paradise of foodies, the walled city of old Lahore, and Lahori cholay, also known as chikar cholay, unquestionably has what it takes.

You can use Lahori cholay as part of any complete Pakistani breakfast—from Halwa Puri Nashta (page 87) to Anda Paratha Qeema (page 88). Some Karachiwalas may prefer their version of chickpea stew for halwa puri breakfast, but we have no issues recommending the Lahori variant.

This stew easily slots in as a vegetarian entree at any meal. It is usually enjoyed with bread (Puri, page 197; Roti, page 181; Naan, page 193; or Paratha, page 184), rarely with rice. In this respect and in the absence of tomatoes as base, it differs from its more globally popular subcontinental cousin, chana masala.

▾▾▾▾▾▾▾▾▾▾▾▾▾▾▾▾▾▾▾▾▾▾▾▾▾▾

- In a bowl mix ginger, garlic, mashed potato, salt, black pepper, baking soda, red pepper flakes, turmeric, and yogurt to form a paste.

- Heat oil in a saucepan to medium heat and add the onions. Fry until golden brown, about 5 to 6 minutes.

- Add the masala-potato paste to the onions and fry for 4 to 5 minutes.

- Add the chickpeas with the liquid. Cook for 5 minutes over medium heat, stirring frequently.

- Add ½ cup water, lower heat to low and simmer for 6 to 8 minutes or until you have the desired consistency.

- If serving as a standalone item (i.e. not as part of a halwa puri brunch), garnish with chilies, eggs, cilantro, and a dash of black pepper.

COCONUT CHICKPEA CURRY ⓥg

¼ cup oil

1 medium onion, finely chopped

1 teaspoon ginger paste

1 teaspoon garlic paste

½ teaspoon Garam Masala (page 215)

1 teaspoon red pepper flakes

1 tablespoon curry powder

1 teaspoon salt (or to taste)

1 (14-ounce) can diced tomatoes

2 (15-ounce) cans chickpeas (garbanzo), drained

1 (13.5-ounce) can coconut milk

8 to 10 curry leaves (optional)

1 tablespoon freshly squeezed lemon juice

1 green onion, green and white parts, finely chopped

This quick and easy chickpea recipe is one of our favorite vegan dishes. The combination of coconut milk, tomatoes, and lemon juice makes this bean curry both creamy and bright. Perfect when accompanied by Plain White Basmati Rice (page 168).

▼▼▼▼▼▼▼▼▼▼▼▼▼▼▼▼▼▼▼▼▼▼▼▼▼▼▼▼▼

PRO TIP

This recipe is very versatile: you can substitute the chickpeas with other beans such as cannellini or red kidney beans. You can also introduce other vegetables such as cubed potatoes or baby spinach into this dish, adding them at the same time as the chickpeas.

- In a Dutch oven, heat the oil over medium heat. Fry the onion until just golden, 5 to 7 minutes.

- Add the ginger, garlic, garam masala, red pepper flakes, curry powder, salt, and 2 tablespoons of water, and cook for 2 to 3 minutes.

- Add the tomatoes and continue to cook until the tomatoes are soft and mushy, and sauce thickens, 8 to 10 minutes.

- Add the chickpeas and cook, stirring, for about 8 to 10 minutes.

- Stir in the coconut milk, curry leaves, if using, and lemon juice, and turn down the heat to low. Cook until thoroughly heated through, 5 to 7 minutes. Don't cook on high as the coconut milk may separate.

- Ladle into a serving bowl, sprinkle with green onions, and serve.

AYESHA CHUNDRIGAR
Animal Activist

WHY WE LOVE AYESHA

A UK-educated journalist, a news reporter, a former BBC news producer, and a once-practicing psychotherapist, Ayesha turned to animal welfare and advocacy in 2013. Today her name is synonymous with animal rights in Pakistan (go ahead, Google it), and we have been fans and supporters of her for many years. Which is why we have been proud to host her on several occasions at our restaurant to highlight her work to others. Her mission is equally about caring for animals, especially working animals as much as it is about instilling empathy and humanity in people through education and advocacy. You might think she is simply rescuing animals, but she is, in fact, saving us all.

CHOSEN CHARITY: ACF ANIMAL RESCUE

Unsurprisingly, the charity that Ayesha would like to have us support through this book is ACF Animal Rescue, her life's work. ACF Ayesha Chundrigar Foundation is a woman-led non-profit that supports the rescue and rehabilitation of abused and injured animals. In addition

to animal welfare, ACF uses education and advocacy to effect social change toward a more compassionate society. It also helps train underprivileged women and men on the humane use of working animals to earn their livelihood.

AYESHA'S MESSAGE: BE WORTHY OF HAVING A FOUNDATION NAMED AFTER YOU

"When I started my social entrepreneurial venture ACF I had no idea what to name it. I had so many ideas on what I wanted to do that I did not want to restrict it to one particular cause. I was passionate about animal rescue but also committed to therapy for women and children. So I figured I would just name it after me, and make myself a person worthy of having a foundation named after her. After all our success in animal welfare, animal rights advocacy, training women and men on working animal best practices, and therapy through animal care, I realize now that living up to my foundation's name is a forever journey. "

A FAVORITE EAT: KHATTI DAAL/TANGY AND SOUR LENTILS

Ayesha's favorite meal is a simple one: "If I were to choose a meal I could have every day, it would be my mother's khatti daal, accompanied by hot rotis and bhindi [okra]," she told us. Most Pakistanis would agree that a well-made khatti daal can vanquish most meat mains.

To create Ayesha's favorite dish at your home, follow our recipe for Tarka Daal (page 159) with one additional step: when the daal is cooked, and before you make the tarka, add 2 tablespoons of imli tamarind paste and 2 tablespoons of lemon juice. Feel free to adjust both ingredients to achieve your desired level of sourness. Finish off with the tarka. Accompany your khatti daal as Ayesha would with Roti (page 181) and Bhindi Masala (page 157).

VII.

CHAWAL-ROTI

$\cdot\diamond\cdot\diamond\cdot\diamond\cdot\diamond\cdot\diamond\cdot\diamond\cdot\diamond\cdot\diamond\cdot\diamond\cdot\diamond\cdot\diamond\cdot\diamond\cdot$

Rice and Bread

BASMATI RICE

The subcontinental way of preparing rice is quite different from the East Asian or Western method. In other cultures, the rice to cooking water ratio is such that little or no water is thrown out, whereas in traditional Pakistani cooking the perfect boiled rice requires several rinse and drain cycles before cooking, and draining excess water after boiling. This stems from the South Asian obsession that no two grains of boiled rice should stick together and not a single grain should be over or under cooked; we enjoy light, fluffy, clump-free rice every time. I see our Italian friends, with their al dente obsession, nodding in sympathy.

MAKES 4 TO 6 SERVINGS
EFFORT ●○○

PLAIN WHITE BASMATI RICE ⓥ
QUICK AND EASY METHOD

2 cups white basmati rice
1 tablespoon unsalted butter
1 teaspoon salt (optional)

This faster method does not require the draining of excess water after boiling.

- In a large bowl, thoroughly wash the rice using cold water, stirring the rice grains with your fingers and draining the water in the sink. Repeat several times until the water runs clear. Soak for 1 hour.

- In a large, thick-bottomed pot, add the washed rice, butter, salt, and 3½ cups of water, and bring to a boil over high heat, then lower heat to medium and continue to cook uncovered, adjusting heat if needed so that the water keeps bubbling but does not boil over.

- Cook until most of the water is absorbed and you can see bubbles along the sides of the pot. Use a spoon to pick up a few grains of rice and test their doneness with your fingertips. Rice grains should feel al dente, i.e., nearly cooked through but not fully cooked. Now turn down the heat to simmer, cover, and steam for 8 to 10 more minutes.

- Once the rice is steamed through and perfectly cooked, open the lid and gently fluff using a fork. Place in a casserole or rice dish and serve steaming hot.

PLAIN WHITE BASMATI RICE Ⓥ
TRADITIONAL METHOD

2 cups white basmati rice
2 teaspoons salt (optional)
1 tablespoon unsalted butter

This classic method takes a bit longer and requires the draining of excess water after boiling. Note that much of the salt will drain out with the excess water in this method.

▼▼▼▼▼▼▼▼▼▼▼▼▼▼▼▼▼▼▼▼▼▼▼▼▼▼▼▼

• In a large bowl, thoroughly wash the rice using cold water, stirring the rice grains with your fingers and draining the water in the sink. Repeat several times until the water runs clear. Soak for 1 hour.

• In a large, thick-bottomed pot, add 8 cups of water and the salt. Turn heat to medium high and bring to a rolling boil.

• When the water starts to boil, add the washed rice and continue to boil over medium-high heat for 8 to 10 minutes, adjusting heat if needed so that the water keeps bubbling but does not boil over.

• Check the rice grains every few minutes to see when the rice grains are al dente, i.e., nearly cooked through but not fully cooked. You can use a spoon to pick up a few grains of rice and test their doneness with your fingertips.

• When the rice grains are nearly cooked, take the pot off the stove and drain the rice into a colander. Let all the excess water drain out.

• Transfer the rice back into the pot and gently stir in the butter.

• Cover tightly and put the pot on the stove over low heat to steam the rice for 8 to 10 more minutes, the final steaming of the rice or *dum*.

• Once the rice is steamed through and perfectly cooked, open the lid and gently fluff using a fork. Place in a casserole or rice dish and serve steaming hot.

AROMATIC YELLOW RICE

For the whole garam masala:

4 peppercorns

1 bay leaf

1 small cinnamon stick

2 cloves

2 black cardamom pods,
   lightly smashed by hand

¼ teaspoon ground turmeric

PRO TIP

Most Pakistani cooks forgo the muslin pouch and add the whole garam masala pieces directly into the water when cooking the rice. Experienced diners know not to bite on whole cloves and cardamoms. You can use the pouch as directed here or boldly go pouchless!

In this variant of the classic basmati, we dress up plain rice with the aroma of whole garam masala and the color of turmeric. The ingredients and method for making plain rice remain the same. We share the ingredients and additional steps needed for this recipe here.

▼▼▼▼▼▼▼▼▼▼▼▼▼▼▼▼▼▼▼▼▼▼▼▼▼▼

MAKE THE WHOLE GARAM MASALA:

- In a small muslin pouch or sachet, add the peppercorns, bay leaf, cinnamon stick, cloves, and cardamom pods, and tie up with the drawstrings.

- Add the whole garam masala pouch and the turmeric to the rice and water when you start to cook the rice using either the traditional or quick and easy method. Remember to fish out the pouch before serving.

SAFFRON AND BUTTER RICE ⓥ
WITH CASHEWS AND CRANBERRIES

1 teaspoon saffron strands

3 tablespoons warm water

¾ stick (6 tablespoons) unsalted butter

4 green onions, white and green parts, finely chopped

½ cup raw unsalted cashews, raw pistachios, or slivered almonds

⅓ cup cranberries, raisins, or Persian barberries

We now take basmati rice to the next level with a rich, aromatic, and flavorful topping. You can up the tartness by substituting Persian barberries for the cranberries or go the sweeter route by replacing them with raisins or sultanas. At Zareen's, we prepare this rice for special caterings and are always overwhelmed by the rave response. We are sure your guests will give you rave reviews too.

The ingredients and method for making plain rice remain the same—you can use our quick and easy method or go the traditional route. We share here only the additional ingredients and steps needed for this recipe.

▼▼▼▼▼▼▼▼▼▼▼▼▼▼▼▼▼▼▼▼▼▼▼▼▼▼▼

- Using a small saucer, steep the saffron in the warm water. Set aside.

- In a frying pan over medium-low heat, melt the butter. Sauté the onions, cashews, and cranberries in the butter until the cashews turn golden and the onions soften, about 2 minutes. Be sure not to overbrown the cashews. Remove from heat and set aside.

- Cook the rice per the plain basmati rice recipe with one change: prior to the final steaming (dum step), sprinkle the saffron water over the cooked rice and spoon the cashew and onion butter evenly over the top. Then proceed with the steaming.

- Prior to serving, fluff the rice to mix well. Serve hot on a rice platter.

PULAO

Pulao, pullao, or palao is a rice dish richer than plain boiled rice and its variants due to the addition of vegetables, meats, and stock. Pulaos are not as heavily spiced and rich as biryanis, falling midway between plain rice and biryani in this respect. But a well-made pulao will give any biryani a run for its money.

MATAR PULAO ⓥ
Rice Pilaf with Peas

Matar a.k.a. peas pulao is arguably the simplest and most common of pulaos. Here, long-grained basmati rice and sweet peas are cooked in a fragrant broth of caramelized onions, cloves, and cardamom. A flavorful and healthy pulao, it works equally well for family meals and formal dinners. Enjoy with any meat or vegetarian main and a raita of your choice.

For the rice:
2 cups basmati rice
6 tablespoons ghee or oil

For the whole garam
  masala medley:
4 peppercorns
1 bay leaf
1 small cinnamon stick
2 cloves
2 black cardamom pods
  (optional)

⅓ cup finely sliced onion
½ teaspoon cumin seeds
1 cup fresh or frozen peas
1 teaspoon salt (or to taste)

- In a large bowl, thoroughly wash the rice using cold water, stirring the rice grains with your fingers, and draining the water in the sink. Repeat several times until the water runs clear.

- Soak rice in water for at least 30 minutes, ideally 1 hour.

- Meanwhile, in a wide, heavy-bottomed pot over medium heat, heat the oil. Add the whole garam masala medley and fry for 1 minute.

- Add the onion and cumin seeds, and fry until the onions turn golden brown, 4 to 6 minutes.

- Add the peas and fry for another 1 to 2 minutes.

- Strain the rice in a colander. Add the rice, salt, and 3½ cups of water to the pot with the peas, onion, and spices.

- Boil over medium heat without covering until most of the water is absorbed and you can see bubbles along the sides of the pot, 8 to 10 minutes. You can use a spoon to pick up a few grains of rice and test their doneness with your fingertips. Rice grains should feel al dente, i.e., nearly cooked through but not fully cooked.

- Reduce the heat to a simmer, place a tight-fitting lid on the pot, and steam for about 10 minutes. This is the same dum step you follow when making plain basmati rice, and it completes the cooking of the rice grains.

- Turn off the heat and let the pulao sit, covered, for another 5 minutes.

- Fluff the rice gently with a fork and serve steaming hot on a rice platter.

VARIATION

ZEERA PULAO / RICE PILAF WITH CUMIN SEED

In this variation of the Matar Pulao recipe, we skip the peas and increase the portions of onions and cumin seeds as follows:

½ cup finely sliced onions
1½ teaspoons cumin seeds

CHICKEN PULAO

Chicken Rice Pilaf

3 cups sela basmati rice

For the broth (Yakhni):
1 small whole chicken,
    skinned and cut into 12
    to 14 pieces (or 3 pounds
    bone-in chicken thighs or
    drumsticks, or 2 pounds
    boneless thighs)
1 small onion, quartered
1 (2-inch) piece fresh ginger,
    chopped
6 to 8 cloves garlic
2 tablespoons fennel seeds
2 tablespoons coriander
    seeds
1 (2-inch) cinnamon stick
5 cloves
2 star anise
2 black cardamom pods
6 whole dried red chilies
1 teaspoon black peppercorns
1½ teaspoons salt

½ cup plain yogurt
¾ cup oil
1 medium onion, thinly sliced
2 teaspoons ginger paste
2 teaspoons garlic paste
1 teaspoon salt
2 teaspoons ground
    coriander
2 teaspoons cumin seeds
½ teaspoon fennel seeds,
    crushed
1 tablespoon Garam Masala
    (page 215)
1 tablespoon red pepper
    flakes
4 whole Thai green chilies
    (optional)
Hot water, as needed

This is the most common Pakistani pulao featuring meat: basmati rice cooked with chicken and an array of spices. Bone-in chicken is used to make a rich broth or "yakhni," in which the rice is slow-cooked, and that is why this dish is also called yakhni pulao. Unlike vegetarian pulaos, which usually serve as dressed-up accompaniments to savory mains, chicken pulao and other meat pulaos are considered main entrees in their own right.

▼▼▼▼▼▼▼▼▼▼▼▼▼▼▼▼▼▼▼▼▼▼▼▼▼▼▼▼

* Rinse sela basmati rice four times in cold tap water, then soak in a bowl of water for at least 2 hours.

* In a Dutch oven, add 6 cups of water, the chicken pieces, and all the ingredients for the chicken broth (yakhni). Bring mixture to a gentle boil on high, then lower to medium heat and cook for about 15 minutes. The chicken should be just cooked but not fork tender. This should yield about 5 cups of broth.

* Strain broth into a bowl. Pick out the chicken pieces and reserve separately. Optionally, also pick out the whole red chilies and add to the reserved chicken.

* In a small bowl, whip yogurt with 3 tablespoons of water using a fork. Set aside.

* In a Dutch oven, heat oil to medium and fry onions until golden brown, about 8 to 10 minutes. Add chicken, whole red chilies, ginger, garlic, salt, coriander, cumin, fennel seeds, garam masala, and red pepper flakes. Stir and cook for about 3 to 4 minutes. Add in yogurt mixture and cook, stirring frequently, for about 5 to 6 minutes.

* Add in 5 cups of broth and the drained sela rice. Mix gently. Increase heat to bring to a boil, then lower heat and cook on medium until the water is mostly absorbed and you can see bubbles around the sides, 8 to 10 minutes. Add in the whole Thai green chilies. With a wide spatula, give a gentle stir to the rice and chicken, careful not to break the rice.

* Cover the pot tightly with aluminum foil and then the lid, and steam 20 minutes on low heat—the dum step. Check to see if the rice is fully cooked. If the rice is undercooked, splash in some hot water, cover, and steam for an additional 5 minutes.

* Serve on a large platter, alongside Kachumar (page 208) and your favorite raita.

ON BIRYANI

A Pakistani food crawl is powered by men marshaling cauldrons and coalpits to produce sublime kormas, kababs, naans, and niharis. But no crawl along commercial streets will get you the best Pakistani biryani. For this you must stroll down residential lanes and call on grandmas in home kitchens.

We encourage you to visit, in particular, the aunties preserving generational recipes for Bohri, Sindhi, Hyderabadi, Lucknowi, and Memoni biryanis. For the present, we will stay with the classic Karachi chicken biryani.

A rich, extra-dry chicken korma with golden potatoes is a worthy dish by itself. Here it is merely the first step. Layers of nearly cooked basmati rice are alternated with chicken korma in a large cauldron. This assembly is perfumed and colored with saffron, pandan flower water, fresh mint, coriander leaves, and caramelized onions, then sealed and steam-cooked for several hours.

Refreshing yogurt raita is both necessary and sufficient to complete a biryani meal. A spoonful of homemade biryani can only be improved by forsaking the spoon. The aroma from your flavor-stained fingers will prolong your post-biryani high. And you shall blissfully conclude that Pakistani matriarchs are the undisputed masters of biryani. All commercial cooks are merely "student biryani" imposters.

KARACHI BIRYANI

For the saffron milk:

½ cup milk

3 tablespoons butter or oil

1 tablespoon pandan
flower (kewra) water

1 teaspoon saffron strands

For the masala paste:

½ cup yogurt

1½ tablespoons ginger paste

1½ tablespoons garlic paste

1 tablespoon ground
coriander

1 tablespoon Garam Masala
(page 215)

2 teaspoons cayenne red
chili powder

2 teaspoons salt

½ teaspoon ground turmeric

For the rice:

3 cups sela (parboiled)
basmati rice

3 tablespoons salt, plus
more as needed

2 (2-inch) cinnamon sticks

1 tablespoon cumin seeds

For the chicken curry:

¾ cup oil or ghee

1 medium onion, thinly sliced

3 medium potatoes, peeled,
cubed, and soaked in water

2 pounds boneless chicken
thighs, cut into 2-inch
chunks

4 Roma tomatoes, finely
chopped

1 tablespoon tomato paste

2 tablespoons lemon juice

½ cup chopped fresh cilantro

½ cup chopped fresh mint

3 serrano green chilies, cut
lengthwise

1 teaspoon Garam Masala
(page 215)

Biryani is not just the most popular rice dish but possibly the most popular specialty food across Pakistani cuisine, eclipsing such heavyweights as nihari, haleem, and the many famed kababs. With each ethnic community in Karachi offering its own unique take on biryani, Karachiwalas often have several top personal favorites. Our recipe here represents the most prevalent biryani across all the biryani hotspots in the city. We call it simply the Karachi biryani. Serve with a side of Kachumar (page 208), Mint-Cucumber Raita (page 202), and a favorite Hari Chutney (page 205).

▼▼▼▼▼▼▼▼▼▼▼▼▼▼▼▼▼▼▼▼▼▼▼▼▼▼▼

MAKE THE SAFFRON MILK:

- In a medium glass or other microwave-safe bowl, add the milk, butter, pandan flower water, and saffron. Microwave for 30 to 40 seconds to melt the butter. Mix and set aside.

MAKE THE MASALA PASTE:

- In a small bowl, mix all the masala paste ingredients together. Set aside.

MAKE THE RICE:

- Rinse the rice five to six times in tap water until the water runs clear.

- In a large bowl, soak the rice in water, covering the rice fully, for at least 2 hours, or ideally overnight. Drain the rice in a colander when ready to use. This step ensures the sela rice remains long and fluffy after boiling and does not clump together.

- In a large Dutch oven, heat 12 cups of water over high heat.

- Add in the salt and stir. The water should have enough salt to taste like sea water so adjust accordingly. Don't worry about oversalting as the rice will absorb just the right amount of salt, and most of the salt will go away when the excess water is drained.

- Add in the cinnamon sticks and cumin seeds.

- When the water comes to a rolling boil, add in the soaked rice.

- Boil uncovered for 5 to 6 minutes on high heat until the rice is nearly done.

MAKE THE CHICKEN CURRY:

- In a separate large heavy pan or Dutch oven, heat the oil on medium and fry the onion until golden brown, 8 to 10 minutes.

- Remove the onions with a strainer or slotted spoon, and drain on a paper towel. Set aside until needed to assemble biryani.

- In the same oil, fry the potatoes until golden brown and half done, about 4 to 5 minutes, and set aside on a separate towel.

- In the same oil, add the chicken and the masala paste, and cook on medium for 4 to 5 minutes, stirring frequently.

- Now add the tomatoes, tomato paste, and ½ cup water. Cook uncovered, stirring occasionally, for about 25 to 30 minutes until the meat is fork tender, the oil separates and rises and about a cup of curry sauce is left in the pot.

- Mix in the fried potatoes and lime juice and cook for another minute, then turn off the heat.

TO ASSEMBLE:

- Preheat the oven to 350 degrees F.

- Spread 1 cup of cooked rice at the bottom of a pan.

- Layer all the chicken curry over the rice. Then layer the rest of the rice on top of the curry.

- Pour the saffron milk in a circle over the rice.

- Sprinkle in the reserved fried onions, cilantro, mint, chilies, and garam masala and cover the pan tightly, first with an aluminum foil sheet and then with the lid.

- Put it in the oven and let it steam for 20 to 25 minutes (the dum method, see page 169).

- Take out of oven. Steam should escape as you remove lid. If not, continue steaming in the oven for another 8 to 10 minutes. Mix with a spatula and fluff rice lightly before serving on a platter.

ROTI ⓥg
Whole Wheat Crepes

½ teaspoon salt

2 cups (480 g) plus ¼ cup wheat flour, plus more as needed

1 ¼ cups of warm water

1 teaspoon unsalted butter or ghee (optional)

PRO TIPS

Be careful not to make the tava too hot or you will get burned, unevenly cooked rotis.

Experiment with the size and thickness of your rotis as you roll them out, to get your desired preference.

You can keep the dough in a sealed container in the fridge for 1 to 2 days. Let it come to room temperature again before using to make fresh rotis.

Roti and its fancier cousins, paratha and naan, are present at nearly every subcontinental meal. Roti is an unleavened flatbread that is made on a stovetop by heating whole wheat "crepes" on a curved cast-iron skillet called a tava (very different from the naan we enjoy at restaurants, which is leavened flatbread cooked in a clay oven called a tandoor). While naans are eagerly greeted by diners eating out, and parathas make their flashy appearances on special occasions, the more faithful but no less fulfilling staple of Pakistani home-cooked meals remains the roti.

▼▼▼▼▼▼▼▼▼▼▼▼▼▼▼▼▼▼▼▼▼▼▼▼▼▼▼

KNEADING THE DOUGH:

* In a large bowl, add the salt to 2 cups of flour and mix.

* Add about ¾ cup of warm water and start to mix by hand to make a dough.

* Slowly add more water a little at a time, and follow the kneading steps on page 183.

* Cover the bowl with plastic wrap or a damp cloth and set aside to rest for at least 20 minutes but ideally more than 1 hour.

ROLLING THE ROTIS:

* Divide the dough into 8 pieces and roll each piece in your palms into a ball. If you prefer thinner, smaller rotis, divide the dough into 10 pieces. Place on a plate and cover with the plastic wrap or a damp cloth.

* Shaping 1 piece at a time (leaving the rest covered), place a dough ball on a clean flat surface (kitchen counter or large cutting board) that is dusted with ¼ cup of wheat flour. Flatten it with your palm to make a 2-to-3-inch disc.

* Using a rolling pin, roll the roti disc out into a thin circle, about 6 inches in diameter. The desired thickness is of a thin pancake about ¼ inch thick. Dust the roti lightly with more wheat flour as needed to prevent it getting stuck to the rolling pin. Roll out a few dough balls into roti discs before you start cooking so you can batch cook several sequentially.

CONTINUED

COOKING THE ROTIS:

- Heat a tava or cast-iron skillet over medium-high heat.
- Brush off any flour from the surface of the roti, then place it carefully on the dry skillet.
- Cook on the first side until the top of the roti just starts to look dry, about 20 seconds. Then flip the roti.
- Continue cooking the roti for another 1 to 2 minutes, until both sides are golden brown and even charred a bit in spots, flipping as needed. At this time, you can help the center puff up by pressing the roti with a cloth, paper towel, or spatula.
- Take the roti off the skillet and brush lightly with butter.
- You can serve the roti piping hot one at a time, or keep them in a tortilla warmer or ziplock bag lined with a paper towel, while the remaining rotis cook before serving.

1 Combine salt, flour, and some of the water, and mix by hand. / 2 Knead with a clenched fist until the flour and water are combined, about 1 to 2 minutes. / 3 Continue kneading for 4 to 6 more minutes by folding the dough over on itself. Add a little more flour if you feel the dough has become too sticky, or more warm water if the dough is too crumbly. / 4 When the dough has become soft and pliable but firm, set aside to rest.

PARATHA ⓥ
Pan-Fried Wheat Flatbread

2 cups (480 g) plus ¼
cup whole wheat flour,
divided, plus more as
needed

½ teaspoon salt

1 ¼ cup lukewarm water,
plus more as needed

9 tablespoons softened
ghee or oil

PRO TIPS

You can swap out ½ cup
of whole wheat flour with
½ cup of maida, sold in
Indian/Pakistani grocery
stores. Close enough
substitutes for maida in the
United States are cake flour
or all-purpose flour. Maida
makes parathas lighter and
flakier.

You can keep the whole
batch of dough in a sealed
container in the fridge for
1 to 2 days. Let it come to
room temperature again
before rolling into balls.

You can also freeze the
rolled-out, uncooked
parathas, putting wax
paper between them.

Adding ghee or oil to the dough and using more during frying transforms the roti into a paratha. Parathas are the go-to bread at brunch or an extra-special breakfast, as well as a savory teatime snack. Indeed, any time from 6 a.m. to 2 a.m. is "chai-paratha" time in Karachi. Our recipe results in a layered, square-shaped paratha, achieved by folding and refolding the rolled-out dough several times. Other shapes—triangular and circular—are also popular, with the multilayer texture being the constant.

PS: A paratha fried in oil is no match for one made and fried with ghee.

▼▼▼▼▼▼▼▼▼▼▼▼▼▼▼▼▼▼▼▼▼▼▼▼▼▼▼

KNEADING THE DOUGH:

- In a large shallow bowl, mix 2 cups of flour and the salt.

- Add about ¾ cup of lukewarm water and start to mix with your hands to make a dough.

- Slowly add more water a little at a time, and follow the kneading steps on page 183.

- Cover with plastic wrap or a damp cloth and set aside to rest for at least 30 minutes.

SHAPING AND ROLLING THE PARATHAS:

- Divide the dough into 6 pieces and roll each piece into a ball.

- Shaping 1 piece at a time, place a dough ball on a surface that is dusted with ¼ cup flour. Flatten it with your palm to make a 2½-to-3-inch disc.

- Using a rolling pin, roll the disc out into a thin circle, about 6 inches in diameter. Dust the dough discs lightly with flour as needed to prevent it getting stuck to the rolling pin.

- Fold the circular paratha into a square, following the steps on page 185.

CONTINUED

1 Fold one side of the paratha a third of the way. / **2** Fold the other side to form a rectangle, brushing with ghee. / **3** Fold rectangle along its length to get a compact, square-ish dough block. **4** Roll out this multilayered dough block into a thin square paratha.

FRYING THE PARATHAS:

• Heat a tava or cast-iron skillet over medium heat. If you fry parathas on high heat, they will char and burn; if on low heat they will absorb the oil and become soggy.

• Gently place a paratha on the dry tava and let it cook for about 1 minute. Using a spoon, add about 1 tablespoon of ghee onto the tava along each of the four sides of the paratha, but not directly on the paratha. Cook for about 1 to 2 minutes, pressing down the sides of the paratha gently.

• Now flip the paratha and cook the other side. If needed, you can spoon about ½ tablespoon of ghee along the sides to aid in the frying.

• Continue cooking the paratha until both sides are a rich golden brown. You may need to flip more than once.

• Parathas are best served piping hot one at a time. But if your family and friends want to wait for you to join them, you can keep the parathas in a tortilla warmer or a paper towel-lined ziplock bag.

MICHELLE TAM
Food Activist

WHY WE LOVE MICHELLE TAM

A doctor of pharmacy from University of California San Francisco and an ICU pharmacist at Stanford Hospital who became a health activist, an award-winning author, and an innovator who brought the world delicious paleo foods. She is the creator of the movement that is Nom Nom Paleo, encompassing a two-time Webby Award-winning cooking app, a Best of Paleo Award-winning podcast, and a James Beard Award-nominated and *New York Times*-bestselling cookbook series. Hailed as the "Martha Stewart of Paleo" by the *New York Times*, Michelle has helped hundreds of thousands of people eat and live better with her food activism. We also love that she loves the food at Zareen's, where she is a regular.

CHOSEN CHARITY: THE WOMEN'S BUILDING

We asked Michelle to nominate a charity she would like us to support through the sales of this book. Michelle chose The Women's Building in San Francisco: a women-led community that advocates for self-determination, gender equality, and social justice. As a safe place focused on women's issues, The Women's Building welcomes 25,000 women and their families each year, connecting them with social services, community involvement opportunities, the arts, wellness, and educational events.

MICHELLE'S MESSAGE: LISTEN TO ACTIONS, NOT ADVICE

"My immigrant parents were not big fans of my decision to leave a stable fourteen-year career at Stanford University Hospital and all my academic training to start a new venture as a food activist. They told me not to make this risky bet, away from stability and security. But they had left their country and traveled thousands of miles, launching their family to an unknown future. So I decided to listen to their actions and not their advice. And Nom Nom Paleo was launched. My impact on home kitchens and dinner tables around the world is the best ROI on my risky bet."

A FAVORITE EAT: PLANTAIN-COATED AIR-FRYER CHICKEN NUGGETS

When asked to pick a well-loved recipe, Michelle chose plantain-coated chicken nuggets, a favorite paleo treat. Coated with crushed plantain chips and cassava flour, and cooked in an air fryer, these healthy chicken bites are paleo friendly, gluten-free, grain-free, nut-free, and irresistible! We happily admit that these plantain-crusted chicken nuggets are one of our family's absolute favorites among the Nom Nom Paleo collection. You can find the full recipe by searching for "Plantain-Coated Air-Fryer Chicken Nuggets" at the Nom Nom Paleo blog NomNomPaleo.com.

When we make these nuggets at our home, we sometimes use cayenne chili powder in place of paprika for an additional kick. And we always enjoy them with our Wicked Spicy Chutney (page 207) and our Garlic-Chili Ketchup (page 207).

LACHHA PARATHA ⓥ
Multilayered Flatbread

1 cup plus ¼ cup all-
   purpose flour
1 cup whole wheat flour
½ cup milk
½ cup plus 2 tablespoons
   softened ghee or oil,
   divided
1 teaspoon sugar
½ teaspoon salt
¼ cup lukewarm water,
   plus more as needed

PRO TIP

Don't apply too much
pressure when you're
rolling out paratha or
you'll lose your layers.

With more layers, a lighter texture, and a sweeter taste, lachha paratha or lacchay-dar paratha takes the addictive comfort of paratha to the next level. The lighter texture comes from the introduction of maida, a finely milled subcontinental flour. If you are not up to buying this from your local Indian/Pakistani grocery store, you can use cake flour, white bread flour, or all-purpose flour. In our recipe we use whole wheat flour (atta) and all-purpose flour (maida substitute) in equal portions.

▾▾▾▾▾▾▾▾▾▾▾▾▾▾▾▾▾▾▾▾▾▾▾▾▾▾

KNEADING THE DOUGH:

- In a large shallow bowl, mix 1 cup of all-purpose flour, the whole wheat flour, milk, 2 tablespoons of ghee, the sugar, and salt.

- Start adding water, a little at a time, and follow the kneading steps on page 183.

- Cover with plastic wrap or a damp cloth and set aside to rest for at least 20 to 30 minutes.

SHAPING THE PARATHAS:

- Divide the dough into 4 pieces, roll each piece into a ball, and cover with plastic wrap or a damp towel. Let rest for 10 minutes.

- Shaping 1 piece at a time, place a dough ball on a surface that is dusted with all-purpose flour and flatten it with your palm to make a 2-to-3-inch disc.

ROLLING THE PARATHAS:

- Using a rolling pin, roll the disc out into a thin crepe, about 8 inches in diameter and about ¼ inch thick. Dust lightly with flour as needed to prevent the discs from getting stuck as you roll.

- Brush the entire surface of the crepe with ghee. Sprinkle with a little flour.

- Follow the steps on page 191 to shape the paratha, i.e. laminate to introduce layers.

CONTINUED

FRYING THE PARATHAS:

- Heat a tava or a skillet over medium heat. If you fry the parathas on high heat, they will char and burn; if on low heat they will absorb the oil and become soggy.

- Gently place a paratha on the dry tava and let it cook for about 30 to 40 seconds. Flip the paratha and cook the other side for about 30 to 40 seconds.

- Now flip the paratha back and use a spoon to add about 1 tablespoon of ghee onto the tava around the edge of the paratha. Cook this side for about 1 minute, pressing down the sides of the paratha gently.

- Flip the paratha one last time and once again use a spoon to add about 1 tablespoon of ghee onto the tava around the edge of the paratha. Keep pressing the sides gently to help puff up the center.

- Continue cooking the paratha until both sides are a rich golden brown.

- Parathas are best served piping hot one at a time. But if your family and friends want to wait for you to join them, you can keep parathas in a tortilla warmer or a paper towel-lined ziplock bag.

1 Pleat crepe by folding the paratha like a paper fan. / 2 Roll the pleated log with your palm to lengthen, then roll it up into a disc. Tuck the ends into the center. 3 Press down on this multilayered "Swiss roll" disc. / 4 Roll out into a thin round paratha.

NAAN ⓥ
Leavened Flatbread

For the dough:
1 cup lukewarm water
½ cup milk powder/
  powdered milk
¼ cup yogurt
3 tablespoons melted salted
  butter
3 teaspoons sugar
1 egg
2 teaspoons active dry yeast
1 teaspoon salt
½ teaspoon baking powder
4 cups all-purpose flour,
  plus more for dusting

*For the milk-water
  paste (optional) for
  basting the pastry:*
2 tablespoons milk powder
¼ cup lukewarm water

*Garnish for sesame
  seed naan:*
3 tablespoons sesame seeds

Garnish for garlic naan:
3 tablespoons minced garlic
3 tablespoons of finely
  chopped fresh cilantro
Oil, for brushing and greasing
Butter, for serving (optional)

While naans are seen as the exclusive domain of restaurants, a crossover to home kitchens is entirely possible without installing a tandoori clay oven in your patio. Our recipe uses a skillet to perform the clay oven wall's function of getting the naan base crispy, and a regular oven to get the naan golden brown. Besides regular naan, we also include instructions here on how to make the two most popular naan variations in Pakistan: sesame seed and garlic.

▼▼▼▼▼▼▼▼▼▼▼▼▼▼▼▼▼▼▼▼▼▼▼▼▼▼▼

KNEADING THE DOUGH:

• In a large bowl, add in lukewarm water, milk powder, yogurt, butter, sugar, egg, yeast, salt, and baking powder. Whisk well.

• Add in the flour and knead the dough, 3 to 5 minutes, into a soft, slightly sticky dough. Follow the kneading steps on page 183.

PROOFING THE DOUGH:

• Cover the bowl with plastic wrap and place in a warm place to proof. This may take anywhere from 60 to 90 minutes depending on the climate.

• Move the oven rack to the center of the oven and set the oven on the Hi Broil setting.

• To prevent dough from sticking, wet your hands with water, then put the proofed dough onto a smooth surface and gently punch down to release the air, if needed. Divide and shape the dough to make 6 to 7 large, equal-size dough balls. Lightly brush the balls with oil and cover with a towel to prevent from drying up. Set aside for 10 to 15 minutes.

MAKE THE MILK-WATER PASTE (OPTIONAL):

• In a small bowl, combine the powdered milk with ¼ cup of water. Set aside.

CONTINUED

ROLLING THE DOUGH:

- Follow the steps on page 195 to roll out the naan dough.

COOKING THE NAAN:

- Heat a skillet over medium heat. When hot, place the back side of the naan on the skillet. After 1 to 2 minutes, check to see if the bottom of the naan has turned golden by lifting the side of the naan with a spatula.

- Using a wide spatula, place the naan in the oven directly on the oven rack or on a greased baking sheet, and broil until golden brown, about 2 minutes.

- Brush the top of the naans with a little butter before serving to help the naans stay soft.

> **VARIATIONS**
>
> If making sesame seed naan or garlic naan, place these garnishes on the naan dough right after you brush the naan dough with the milk-water paste and just before placing the naan on a heated skillet:
>
> **SESAME SEED NAAN:** Sprinkle about ½ tablespoon of sesame seeds evenly over the top of each naan.
>
> **GARLIC NAAN:** Add about ½ tablespoon of minced garlic and ½ table-spoon of chopped fresh cilantro evenly over the top of each naan.

1 Divide dough into equal-size dough balls. / 2 Roll out the ball into a 6- to 7-inch disc.
3 Brush naan top with milk-water paste. / 4 (optional) Sprinkle sesame seeds over each naan.

PURI (Vg)

Puffy Fried Bread

2 cups (240 g) all-purpose
   flour
½ teaspoon salt
½ cup plus 2 tablespoons
   lukewarm water
¼ cup oil for brushing
   dough balls
Oil, for rolling and
   deep-frying

Unlike rotis and regular parathas, puris are made partly or
wholly with maida all-purpose flour instead of atta whole wheat
flour. Our recipe uses maida exclusively, but you can use equal
parts whole wheat and all-purpose flour if you want. A platter
of crispy, flaky, steaming hot, puffed-up puris surpass all rotis,
naans, and parathas for visual, gustatory, and olfactory appeal.

▼▼▼▼▼▼▼▼▼▼▼▼▼▼▼▼▼▼▼▼▼▼▼▼▼▼▼▼

KNEADING THE DOUGH:

* In a large shallow bowl, add the flour and salt, and mix.

* Add about ½ cup water and mix with your hands to make a crumbly dough, about 1 minute.

* Slowly add more water and follow the kneading steps on page 183.

ROLLING THE PURIS:

* Divide the dough into 7 to 8 pieces and roll each piece in your
  palms into a ball.

* Place the dough balls in a wide dish. Brush the balls generously
  with oil. Cover with plastic wrap and let rest in a warm place for
  30 to 40 minutes.

* Using a rolling pin on a smooth surface, roll each disc out into a
  thin puri about 5 inches in diameter.

DEEP-FRYING THE PURIS:

* Heat 4 inches of oil in a wok or karahi. When the oil reaches a
  temperature of 350 degrees F or passes the wooden spoon test
  (see page 32), it is ready for deep-frying.

* Slide a puri into the oil. Fry while very gently pressing it using
  the back of a slotted spatula. It should puff up right away, if the
  temperature is correct. When the puri puffs up, its bottom side is
  light golden, and no more bubbles are forming, flip it over.

* Fry the other side until it's a pale golden color. It should only
  take 30 to 60 seconds per side; don't fry too long, otherwise the
  puri will become too brown and crispy. The perfect puri is flaky,
  crispy, and a little soft on the inside.

* Remove the puri and place on a paper towel-lined plate. Repeat
  with the rest of the puris.

* Serve the puris while still puffed and steaming hot.

VIII

IZAFI

✦•✦•✦•✦•✦•✦•✦•✦•✦•✦•✦•✦•✦

On the Side

RAITAS
Seasoned Yogurt Dips

Raita is the ever-present accompaniment to nearly all Pakistani mains, especially those featuring kababs, fried items, rice dishes, and drier curries and stews.

The raita's cooling power perfectly tempers the inherent heat of many Pakistani dishes. Its cooling function notwithstanding, you can add a bit of heat to your raita by mixing in a pinch or two of cayenne red chili powder or some finely chopped fresh green chilies—or by using these as garnishes.

Here we provide the basic recipe plus several popular variations.

MAKES 4 SERVINGS
EFFORT ● ○ ○

PLAIN RAITA ⓥ

1 cup yogurt
1 clove garlic, crushed and minced
2 to 3 tablespoons water
¼ teaspoon freshly ground black pepper
¼ teaspoon cumin seeds (optional)
¼ teaspoon salt
½ tablespoon finely chopped fresh mint or cilantro, plus more for garnish (optional)

PRO TIP

You can store plain raita tightly covered in the refrigerator for 3 days.

Our not-so-plain take on the basic raita version pumps up the zing with crushed garlic alongside staple raita ingredients, cumin, and black pepper.

- In a medium bowl, add all the ingredients and whisk thoroughly until smooth.
- Transfer to a serving dish. Garnish with fresh herbs and serve.

CUCUMBER RAITA ⓥ

For the raita base:

1 cup plain yogurt

¼ to ½ teaspoon freshly
ground black pepper

¼ to ½ teaspoon salt

¼ teaspoon cumin seeds

3 Persian cucumbers, finely
diced or grated

1 tablespoon finely chopped
fresh mint or cilantro plus
more for garnish (optional)

PRO TIPS

You can use an English
cucumber instead of
Persian cucumbers.

We don't add additional
water in this raita as the
cucumber will release
water and make the raita
a thinner consistency. You
can add a little water if
you prefer.

Use up this refreshing
side in 1 to 2 days. With
the cucumber releasing
its water, this raita does
not keep as well in the
fridge as plain raita.

Alternately silken and crunchy in texture, and always deliciously cooling, cucumber raita is the perfect side for spicier
mains. Varying the proportions of the mint and adding cilantro
gives you two popular variations.

▾▾▾▾▾▾▾▾▾▾▾▾▾▾▾▾▾▾▾▾▾▾▾▾▾▾▾▾

MAKE THE RAITA BASE:

- In a medium bowl, whisk the yogurt, ¼ teaspoon pepper, ¼ teaspoon salt, and the cumin seeds until smooth. Taste and add an
additional ¼ teaspoon of salt and pepper if needed.

- Add the cucumbers and mint or cilantro and mix well.

- Serve in a small bowl, garnished with fresh herbs.

VARIATIONS

MINT-CUCUMBER RAITA: Prepare the cucumber raita per the recipe,
adding 2 tablespoons of finely chopped fresh mint *or* 1 teaspoon of
dried mint leaves when whisking the yogurt.

CILANTRO-CUCUMBER RAITA: Prepare the cucumber raita per the
recipe, adding 2 tablespoons of finely chopped fresh cilantro when
whisking the yogurt.

BEET RAITA ⓥ

1 medium beet
1 recipe raita base from
Cucumber Raita (page 202)
1 tablespoon finely chopped
fresh mint for garnish
(optional)

This raita is just as deliciously cooling but far more colorful than cucumber raita. Use all the same ingredients in the recipe for Cucumber Raita, replacing only the Persian cucumber with half of a medium beet.

▼▼▼▼▼▼▼▼▼▼▼▼▼▼▼▼▼▼▼▼▼▼▼▼▼▼▼

- In a medium saucepan, add the beet and enough water to cover, and boil until fully cooked, 20 to 25 minutes. Let it cool.
- Peel the beet (the skin should slip off easily) and cut in half.
- Dice half of the beet for the raita; save the other half for other use.
- Add the diced beet into the prepared raita base and mix well.
- Garnish with mint and serve.

HARA RAITA ⓥ

Mint-Cilantro "Green" Raita

1 cup plain yogurt
2 to 3 tablespoons Hari
Chutney (page 205)
Pinch of salt, plus more
as needed
½ tablespoon chopped
fresh cilantro (optional)

A personal favorite, this herb-infused yogurt dip is made by cooling down the intense flavors of the Hari Chutney (page 205) with yogurt. Note the absence of cumin or black pepper that typically flavor other raitas, and the lower amount of added salt since the chutney is already salty.

▼▼▼▼▼▼▼▼▼▼▼▼▼▼▼▼▼▼▼▼▼▼▼▼▼▼▼

- In a medium bowl, whisk the yogurt, 2 tablespoons of chutney, 1 tablespoon of water, and a pinch of salt together until they are mixed well. Taste and add another tablespoon of chutney and more salt if desired. If the consistency is too thick, add another tablespoon of water and mix.
- Transfer to a serving dish and garnish with cilantro.

CHUTNEYS

Chutneys are popular dipping sauces that accompany main dishes. Many home-cooked meals will have a raita, one or more chutneys, and a kachumar side. Chutneys typically have a lemon-and-water base, not a yogurt base, as is the case with raitas and so they store well in the fridge for several days.

MAKES 4 SERVINGS
EFFORT ●○○

HARI CHUTNEY ⓥg
Mint-Cilantro "Green" Chutney

2 cups coarsely chopped fresh cilantro

1 cup coarsely chopped fresh mint

1 serrano chili, finely chopped, deseed to reduce heat

2 tablespoons of freshly squeezed lemon juice

2 garlic cloves

1 tablespoon vinegar

1 teaspoon sugar

1 teaspoon cumin seeds

4 to 5 ice cubes

½ teaspoon salt

The most popular chutney in Pakistani cuisine by far is the hari green chutney. To put a spin on this classic, try blending one ripe tomato with the ingredients below for a refreshingly acidic kick.

▾▾▾▾▾▾▾▾▾▾▾▾▾▾▾▾▾▾▾▾▾▾▾▾▾▾▾

PRO TIP

The ice cubes keep the chutney ingredients cool during blending, helping it retain its vibrant green color.

- In a blender, add the cilantro, mint, chili, lemon juice, garlic, vinegar, sugar, cumin seeds, ice cubes, and salt, and blend until smooth.

- Serve on the side in a shallow bowl.

HARI CHUTNEY WITH ANARDANA Ⓥ

Mint-Cilantro Chutney with Pomegranate Seeds

1 cup chopped fresh mint
½ cup chopped fresh cilantro
1 serrano chili
¼ small onion
1 large tomato
2 cloves garlic
1 tablespoon ground dried pomegranate seeds
1 teaspoon roasted and crushed cumin seeds (page 47 in The Desi Pantry)
½ teaspoon salt

Boldly going where no green chutney has ever gone before, this recipe ups the tanginess factor by adding pomegranate seeds and tomato. This is our favorite dip for fried fish and crispy fried chicken.

▼▼▼▼▼▼▼▼▼▼▼▼▼▼▼▼▼▼▼▼▼▼▼▼▼

- In a blender, add all the ingredients and blend until smooth. Add 3 tablespoons of water if necessary to get a smooth texture.

IMLI CHUTNEY Ⓥ

Tamarind Chutney

½ cup (4 ounces) seedless tamarind cut from a compressed tamarind slab
½ cup sugar
2 tablespoons white vinegar
1 teaspoon salt
½ teaspoon ground ginger
½ teaspoon cayenne red chili powder
¼ teaspoon ground cinnamon or nutmeg (optional)

PRO TIP

Instead of mixing seedless tamarind from a slab with water, you can substitute ½ cup of premade store-bought tamarind paste.

A popular sweet-and-sour dip, imli tamarind chutney is the go-to side for all barbecue and kabab specialties and many savory snacks, pakoras, samosas, and chaats. You can buy the "compressed" tamarind slab required in this recipe at any Indian/Pakistani store, some specialty grocery stores, many supermarkets, and, of course, on Amazon.

▼▼▼▼▼▼▼▼▼▼▼▼▼▼▼▼▼▼▼▼▼▼▼▼▼

- In a blender, add the tamarind to 1 cup of water and blend to form a tamarind paste.
- In a small saucepan, add the tamarind paste, 2 cups of water, and all the other ingredients. Cook on medium heat for 15 to 20 minutes, stirring occasionally, until the chutney is thick and syrupy in consistency.
- Take off the stove and allow to cool before serving.

WICKED SPICY CHUTNEY

½ bunch cilantro
½ bunch mint
3 serrano chilies
4 cloves garlic
½ cup chopped onion
½ cup ketchup
1 tablespoon tamarind paste
1 teaspoon salt
½ teaspoon cayenne red
    chili powder

A favorite topping for the rolls, sliders, and burgers served at Zareen's restaurants, our house-made wicked spicy chutney is one of our hotter condiments, out-punching imli chutney and all hari chutney variants, and trailing only the Red Hot Garlic-Chili Chutney (page 207) on the hellraiser scale.

- In a blender, blend all the ingredients until smooth.
- Transfer to a small saucepan. Cook the mixture on medium heat for 8 to 10 minutes, until it thickens to a smooth, syrupy consistency and has a rich reddish-brown color.
- Take off the stove and allow to cool before serving.

RED HOT GARLIC-CHILI CHUTNEY ⓥg

1 cup dried red chilies
Warm water, for soaking
¼ cup white vinegar
¼ cup oil
½ tablespoon cumin seeds
1 teaspoon salt
1 teaspoon sugar
5 cloves garlic

Move over sriracha, this is by far the hottest chutney at Zareen's and the favorite condiment of our more adventuresome diners. Serve with your favorite Pakistani—and non-Pakistani—rolls, sliders, and burgers, or as a side condiment to fried and barbecued items.

- In a medium bowl, soak the chilies in warm water for 1 hour or so to soften. Discard the soaking water.
- Transfer the rehydrated chilies and all the other ingredients to a blender, and blend until smooth.

VARIATION

GARLIC-CHILI KETCHUP: Skip the oil and add in ½ cup of ketchup in the garlic-chili chutney recipe to get garlic-chili ketchup.

KACHUMAR ⓥ
Chopped Tomato-Onion Salad

1 cup finely chopped
vine-ripe tomato

1 cup finely chopped red or
yellow onion

¾ cup finely chopped
fresh cilantro

½ cup chopped Persian
cucumber

1 to 2 serrano chilies, finely
chopped (deseed to
reduce heat)

3 tablespoons freshly
squeezed lemon juice

¼ to ½ teaspoon salt

¼ teaspoon freshly ground
black pepper

¼ teaspoon cayenne red
chili powder (optional)

PRO TIPS

Feel free to vary the
onion-tomato-cucumber
proportions.

Reduce or increase the
green chili per your heat
preference.

Kachumar does give off
water, so it only keeps for
1 to 2 days in the fridge.

The meat-loving Pakistani's concession to salad, kachumar or
kachumbar is the refreshing, ever-present side accompanying all biryanis and kababs. Family resemblance to its Latin
cousin, salsa fresca, is striking, with the addition of cucumber
and the slightly higher onion-to-tomato ratio in kachumar
being the notable differences.

▾▾▾▾▾▾▾▾▾▾▾▾▾▾▾▾▾▾▾▾▾▾▾▾▾▾▾

- In a medium serving bowl, mix together the tomato, onion, cilantro, cucumber, and chilies.

- Mix in the lemon juice, ¼ teaspoon of salt, the black pepper, and
  cayenne. Taste and add another ¼ teaspoon of salt if needed.
  Mix well and serve.

KARACHI-STYLE COLESLAW (V)

½ cup mayonnaise

½ cup heavy cream

2 tablespoons sugar

½ tablespoon white vinegar

Pinch of salt, plus more as needed

Pinch of freshly ground black pepper, plus more as needed

4 cups (14 ounces) shredded green cabbage

Pinch of paprika or cayenne red chili powder (optional)

PRO TIP

You can substitute half-and-half for the heavy cream.

We like to substitute Miracle Whip in place of mayonnaise. If you do so, reduce the amount of sugar to 1½ tablespoons.

Crunchy and creamy, sweet and sour but mostly sweet, this is the coleslaw us Karachiwalas grew up on. It works well as a much-needed cooling sideshow to Memoni Crispy Fried Chicken (page 95), spicy Paratha Rolls (page 73), Bun Kabab (page 70), and other hot attractions.

▼▼▼▼▼▼▼▼▼▼▼▼▼▼▼▼▼▼▼▼▼▼▼▼▼▼▼

- In a large bowl, whisk the mayonnaise, cream, sugar, vinegar, salt, and pepper together.

- Add the cabbage and toss well. Taste and adjust salt, pepper, and sugar as needed.

- Chill in the fridge for 1 hour or more.

- Garnish with a dash of paprika, then serve.

MEMONI CARROT ACHAR

Spicy Carrot Pickle

2 tablespoons coriander
seeds

1 teaspoon yellow mustard
seeds

1 clove of garlic, crushed
and minced

5 tablespoons oil

1 tablespoon cayenne red
chili powder

½ teaspoon salt

2 medium carrots, peeled
and julienned

This "instant" achar or quick pickle is a family recipe and
a personal favorite. It goes especially well with lentils and
vegetarian dishes, accompanies barbecue items, and adds a
punch to weekend brunch.

▼▼▼▼▼▼▼▼▼▼▼▼▼▼▼▼▼▼▼▼▼▼▼▼▼▼▼▼

PRO TIPS

You can lower the heat level by reducing the amount of cayenne pepper.

Feel free to add in thinly sliced green mango, radishes, sliced bell pepper,
or green chilies.

If you use up the carrot in your prepared achar but still have the chili masala oil left, top up with more carrot sticks or use other vegetables.

This keeps in the fridge for about 1 week.

- With a mortar and pestle, pound the coriander seeds coarsely
  or grind in a coffee grinder. Transfer to a medium bowl and
  set aside.

- Add the mustard seeds to the mortar and use the pestle to
  pound coarsely or grind in a coffee grinder. Add to the same
  medium bowl.

- In the bowl, add the garlic, oil, cayenne, and salt, and mix
  thoroughly.

- Toss this masala with carrot sticks and your achar is ready!

HOMEMADE SPICE MIXES

No store-bought box of chaat masala or garam masala can equal the unadulterated aroma and flavor of its homemade rival. The two recipes below are quick and simple: a two-step dry-roast-then-grind process that takes less than ten minutes and gives you homemade spice mixes that keep well at room temperature for months. In each case, the aromatherapy is an unexpected bonus.

MAKES ABOUT ¼ CUP
EFFORT ●○○

CHAAT MASALA ⓥ

¼ cup coriander seeds
¼ cup cumin seeds
6 dried cayenne red chilies
6 cloves
½ tablespoon salt
1 teaspoon carom seeds
1 teaspoon ground ginger
1 teaspoon dried mango powder
½ teaspoon black salt
¼ teaspoon citric acid

You can buy chaat masala at any Indian/Pakistani grocery store. Or you can make your own chaat masala at home in ten minutes, eliminating fillers and elevating the taste game. Chaat masala is the essential magic dust on all chaats fruit chaat, cholay chaat as well as many savory snacks including pakoras and samosas.

- In a tava or cast-iron skillet, dry roast the coriander and cumin seeds, chilies, and cloves on low heat for 5 to 6 minutes, stirring occasionally, until they turn lightly brown and fragrant.

- Transfer the roasted spices to a coffee grinder and add all the other ingredients. Grind until smooth. Alternatively, you can pound all ingredients with a mortar and pestle.

- Store in a sealed jar at room temperature.

GARAM MASALA ⓥ

¼ cup coriander seeds
2 tablespoons cumin seeds
1 teaspoon cloves
1 teaspoon black
    peppercorns
6 pieces star anise
5 pieces mace
½ nutmeg
2 cinnamon sticks
8 green cardamom pods
4 black cardamom pods

Like chaat masala, garam masala is also readily available in Indian/Pakistani grocery stores. But most Pakistani home cooks prefer to make their own garam masala. Don't worry if one or two of the ingredients below are missing from your pantry: your homemade batch will still be superior to its store-bought rival. Most Pakistani meat curries and kababs feature garam masala as an ingredient or a garnish, vegetable dishes less so.

▼▼▼▼▼▼▼▼▼▼▼▼▼▼▼▼▼▼▼▼▼▼▼▼▼▼▼

- On a tava or cast-iron skillet, dry roast all the ingredients on low heat for 5 to 6 minutes, stirring frequently, until they release their rich aroma.

- Enjoy several minutes of aromatherapy, then transfer the roasted spices to a coffee grinder and grind to a fine powder or pound with a mortar and pestle.

- Continue the aromatherapy session for a minute or two more; then store in a sealed jar at room temperature.

IX.

MASHROOB

❖❖❖❖❖❖❖❖❖❖❖❖❖

Drink Me

MANGO LASSI ⓥ

Yogurt Smoothie

1 cup heavy cream
1 cup whole milk
2 cups ice cubes
3 cups canned mango pulp
½ cup yogurt
½ cup sugar

A light, refreshing, savory drink? Or a creamy, dessert-in-a-glass smoothie? Yes. Lassi is as popular in Pakistan as it is versatile. Here we share our favorite savory and sweet variants of this famous subcontinental beverage.

▼▼▼▼▼▼▼▼▼▼▼▼▼▼▼▼▼▼▼▼▼▼▼▼▼▼▼▼

• Put all ingredients in a blender and blitz together. Serve chilled.

VARIATIONS

SALTED LASSI: 2 cups ice cubes, 1 cup cold water, plus more as needed, 1 cup yogurt, ¼ teaspoon salt, generous pinch of cumin seeds (optional).

SWEET LASSI: 2 cups ice cubes, 2 cups heavy cream or half-and-half, 1 cup whole milk, ½ cup sugar.

ROSE LASSI: 1 cup heavy cream or half-and-half, 1 cup whole milk, 2 cups ice cubes, ½ cup yogurt, ½ cup rose syrup such as Rooh Afza, ½ teaspoon green cardamom, or 4 cardamom pods, crushed

ON KASHMIRI CHAI

❖·❖

King Lear did not relish his daughter's sentiment that she loved him as much as salt. Therefore, King Lear was likely not a fan of Kashmiri chai. Fate, as we know, did not smile kindly on his poor taste.

Kashmiri chai also known as namkeen chai or noon chai is a savory tea that has a pink saltiness instead of the tan sweetness of regular Pakistani chai. Special tea leaves, baking soda, and salt all combine to crown Kashmiri chai as the queen of the subcontinental teascape.

You can add some crushed nuts and, while the purists look away, a dash of sugar. But keep it subtle; overloading Kashmiri chai with sugar would be a Shakespearean tragedy.

KASHMIRI CHAI ⓥ
Kashmiri Pink Tea

*For the tea concentrate
(kahwa):*

4 cups cold water

¼ cup Kashmiri tea leaves

½ teaspoon baking soda

½ teaspoon salt

4 cardamom pods

2 cups ice water or 1 cup
water with 12 to 14 ice
cubes

3 cups whole milk

Sugar, for sweetening
(optional)

2 teaspoons crushed raw
pistachios (optional)

PRO TIPS

You can make the tea con-
centrate in bigger batches
and store in a closed container in the fridge. It should
keep well for 1 week. Then
you can prepare individual
cups of Kashmiri chai any
time the mood strikes.

For a sweeter version, use
less salt (¼ teaspoon versus
½ teaspoon) and add sugar
to taste in the teacup.

The traditional method for making Kashmiri chai requires a
bicep-taxing aeration process in which a ladle is used to alternately take some tea out and pour it back into the saucepan
from a great height during brewing. Our recipe saves time and
the cardio workout but still achieves the pink creaminess of
Kashmiri chai.

▾▾▾▾▾▾▾▾▾▾▾▾▾▾▾▾▾▾▾▾▾▾▾▾▾▾▾

MAKE THE TEA CONCENTRATE KAHWA:

* In a medium saucepan, add the cold water, tea leaves, baking
  soda, salt, and cardamom pods. Don't heat the water before
  adding in the ingredients.

* Turn on the heat and bring mixture to a boil, then reduce heat
  to low.

* Let the tea mixture simmer, stirring occasionally, for about
  20 minutes. The tea mixture should reduce to about 2 cups
  in volume.

* Pour the ice water into the tea mixture. Turn the heat to medium
  high and brew for another 8 to 10 minutes, stirring occasionally.
  If you wish, you can use a ladle to take some tea out and pour it
  back in the saucepan a few times from a height, aerating the tea
  as it brews.

* Remove from heat and pour the mixture through a sieve to take
  out the tea leaves and cardamom pods. You should now have
  about 3 cups of the tea concentrate.

* While the tea concentrate is brewing, heat the milk over low heat
  in a heavy-bottomed saucepan and simmer for 15 to 20 minutes,
  until the milk sugars caramelize and the milk gets a slight creamy-
  beige tint. Make sure to stir frequently so the milk doesn't burn.

* To serve, combine the hot milk and tea concentrate in individual
  cups. The ratio is flexible; we recommend ½ cup milk with ½ cup
  tea concentrate; adjust as desired.

* Lightly sweeten the tea with sugar, and garnish with about ½ teaspoon of crushed pistachios.

RUPI KAUR
Poet

WHY WE LOVE RUPI

Punjabi-Canadian poet, artist, author, and performer, Rupi Kaur has enthralled millions with her poems on love, loss, trauma, healing, femininity, and the immigrant experience. Her poetry collections—*Milk and Honey*, *The Sun and her Flowers*, and *Home Body*—have sold over 11 million copies, spent endless weeks on the *New York Times* bestseller list, and have been translated into over 43 languages. Unlike our other favorite trailblazers spotlighted in this book, Rupi may never have visited Zareen's in person, but she and her poems are ever present in our restaurants, in our homes, and within us.

CHOSEN CHARITY: KHALSA AID

Rupi's chosen charity is Khalsa Aid, an international NGO that provides humanitarian aid in disaster areas and civil conflict zones: from victims of the Yemen Civil War to refugees landing in Greece from the Middle East, to the Rohingya Muslims from Myanmar seeking refuge in Bangladesh. Its mission is based upon the Sikh principle "recognize the whole human race as one."

RUPI'S MESSAGE: FEED YOUR SOUL SO YOU CAN FEED THE WORLD'S

"Sitting around a dinner table eating a home-cooked meal has always been an act of self-care for me. Food connects me to places and people. It centers me in the now. Beyond providing sustenance, a good meal nourishes my body and my soul. It fills my heart. One of my favorite dishes growing up was my mom's Sarson Ka Saag. To this day, it's the dish my soul craves whenever life gets too hard or too hectic. It transports me to my childhood by filling me with a sense of home, and by the end of the meal I feel nourished."

A FAVORITE EAT: SARSON KA SAAG / SPICY MUSTARD GREENS STEW

Rupi's favorite eat is Sarson Ka Saag, a hearty, spicy, stew of mustard greens. It is the comfort food of choice in both Indian Punjab and Pakistani Punjab. Topped with a generous dollop of homemade butter, it is usually enjoyed with Makkai Roti (Maize flour flatbread) never with rice.

Here is a quick and easy recipe for Sarson Ka Saag: In a Dutch oven, add 3 cups of water, 1 (15-ounce) packet of chopped frozen mustard greens, 1 (8-ounce) packet of chopped frozen spinach, 1 tablespoon of coarsely chopped ginger, 5 cloves of garlic, 3 serrano green chilis, and salt to taste. Bring to a boil, then simmer on low heat until the greens are cooked through. Puree the stew in place using an immersion blender. Mix in a tablespoon of dried fenugreek leaves and leave on simmer.

Prepare and add a Tarka (page 159). Garnish with julienned spinach and two tablespoons of butter. Serve with Makkai Maize flour roti, corn tortillas, or regular roti (page 181) and a side of pickles such as Memoni Carrot Achar (page 212).

DOODH PATTI CHAI ⓥ

Milk Tea

6 tea bags, or 5 teaspoons of loose-leaf black tea

½ teaspoon of finely chopped fresh ginger

5 green cardamom pods, cracked open

1½-inch cinnamon stick (optional)

3 cups milk

6 to 8 teaspoons sugar (or to taste)

PRO TIPS

Tea bags or loose-leaf tea? We prefer loose-tea, but frankly both work. Either way, choose Tapal, PG Tips, or a similar strong black tea.

You lose about 1 cup or more of water in the slow-brewing; hence the 6 cups of liquid for 4 servings of tea in our recipe.

Always have 1 to 2 tea bags more than the servings: so 5 to 6 tea bags for 4 servings.

To go richer and creamier, replace some or all of the water with additional milk.

The chai at Zareen's restaurant is famous for fueling friend reunions, first dates, venture dealmaking, and family outings. It is also known for causing minor riots when it runs out. As it takes time to slow-brew the perfect cup of traditional Pakistani doodh patti chai milk tea, there are no shortcuts to refilling our tea station if we run out (hence the riots). The recipe here is faithful to the way milk tea is made in Pakistan, going easy on spices, as opposed to the more pungent, if more popular, stateside masala chai.

▾▾▾▾▾▾▾▾▾▾▾▾▾▾▾▾▾▾▾▾▾▾▾▾▾▾▾▾

- In a large pot over high heat, bring 3 cups of water to a boil.

- Add the tea, ginger, cardamom, cinnamon, and sugar; then reduce the heat to low and brew for about 8 to 10 minutes.

- Stir in the milk, increase heat to medium and cook until the milk starts to froth, another 3 to 5 minutes.

- Reduce heat to simmer and continue to brew for another 8 to 10 minutes.

- Strain to get rid of the tea bags and whole spices, and serve hot.

FALOODA ⓥ

Rose Milkshake with Toppings

3 tablespoons basil seeds
(or chia seeds)

1 (50-gram) package falooda
noodles

1 (3-ounce) package raspberry
or strawberry instant gelatin

2 cups half-and-half

3 tablespoons rose syrup
such as Rooh Afza

¼ teaspoon ground cardamom

3 scoops Rose Ice Cream
(page 243)

1 can whipped cream

1 tablespoon finely chopped
raw pistachios

PRO TIP

Instead of preparing the gelatin using an instant gelatin
mix, you can use premade
Jell-O cups.

Falooda is an adaptation of the Persian dessert faloodeh and
was brought to the Indian subcontinent during the Mughal
period. It is a rose-flavored milkshake, best served with a
scoop of rose petal ice cream, topped with jelly, basil seeds,
and cornstarch vermicelli. Our falooda is based on the award-
winning kulfi falooda served at Baloch Ice Cream shops
in Karachi.

▼▼▼▼▼▼▼▼▼▼▼▼▼▼▼▼▼▼▼▼▼▼▼▼▼▼▼▼

- In a small bowl, soak the basil seeds with ½ cup of water. Mix and
  set aside for 20 minutes.

- In a medium saucepan, bring about 4 cups of water to a boil,
  then add the falooda noodles. Boil the noodles until soft, about
  2 minutes. Strain, add to a bowl of cold water, and keep in fridge
  until ready to use.

- Follow the instructions on the instant gelatin package to make
  the raspberry jelly. Set aside.

- In a medium bowl, mix the half-and-half with the rose syrup and
  cardamom to sweeten it. Keep in the fridge to chill until needed.

- To serve: In a long, narrow glass, add 2 tablespoons of jelly,
  3 tablespoons of falooda noodles, ⅔ cup of sweetened half-and-
  half, and 1 tablespoon of basil seeds. Add a big scoop of rose ice
  cream. Top with some whipped cream and garnish with pistachios and a light drizzle of rose syrup.

MEETHA

·•·◦·•·◦·•·◦·•·◦·•·◦·•·◦·•·◦·•·◦·•·

The Sweet Life

FIRNI ⓥ

Creamy Rice Pudding with Cardamom and Saffron

⅓ cup basmati rice

4 cups whole milk

Half of a 14-ounce can condensed milk

1 teaspoon rose water (optional)

½ teaspoon ground cardamom

Pinch of saffron (optional)

1 tablespoon crushed raw pistachios

1 tablespoon slivered almonds (optional)

Every cuisine has its take on rice pudding. Firni is ours. This creamy, velvety pudding is made with ground rice and scented with saffron, pandan, and green cardamom. Firni's cousin, kheer, differs only in having whole grains of rice, not ground rice, as the principal ingredient. The custardy smoothness and firmness of firni makes it our rice pudding of choice, but you can vary this recipe to make kheer with whole grain rice whenever the fancy strikes you.

▼▼▼▼▼▼▼▼▼▼▼▼▼▼▼▼▼▼▼▼▼▼▼▼▼▼▼▼

- Rinse the rice a few times in water until water runs clear, then soak in water just covering the rice for 1 hour. Drain water before use.

- In a blender, add the rice and ¼ cup of the milk and blend to a smooth paste: the rice grains should be ground very fine. Set aside.

- In a heavy-bottomed pot, heat the remaining milk on medium high until the milk comes to a gentle boil.

- Add in the ground rice and milk paste and stir well. Allow pudding to come to a gentle boil again before lowering the heat to medium low. Now cook uncovered for about 20 minutes, stirring occasionally, until the rice is fully cooked and the pudding has reached a custardy consistency.

- Reduce the heat to low and add the condensed milk. Stir and mix well.

- Add the rose water, cardamom, and saffron, and stir. Cook on low heat for another 6 to 8 minutes. Taste and adjust sweetness by adding more condensed milk if desired.

- Cool in the fridge before serving in individual dessert bowls, garnished with the pistachios and almonds.

VARIATION

KHEER (WHOLE RICE PUDDING WITH CARDAMOM AND SAFFRON)

Follow the Firni recipe with the following changes: do not grind rice; instead cook rice separately in about 1 cup water, making it soft and mushy. Add cooked rice to the boiling milk as in the Firni recipe.

SHEER KHURMA Ⓥ

Roasted Vermicelli Pudding

½ cup slivered raw almonds

½ cup slivered raw pistachios

½ cup yellow or red raisins (optional)

2 tablespoons unsalted butter

1 gallon whole milk

1 (150-gram) package roasted vermicelli (we prefer the Shan brand)

2 (14-ounce) cans condensed milk

3 to 4 tablespoons sugar (or to taste), optional

1 teaspoon ground cardamom

1 teaspoon pandan flower (kewra) water

The festival of Eid marks the end of Ramadan, the month of fasting for Muslims. After thirty days of fasting, the Eid breakfast in Pakistan is highlighted by sheer khurma, a sweet roasted vermicelli pudding. This is repeated at lunch and at dinner, and across all meals on the second day of Eid. And even on the third and final day.

For many Pakistanis, these nine-plus servings of sheer khurma are not enough and we start the sheer khurma marathon on the night before Eid, when we gather for Chand Raat (New Moon Night) celebrations. Thousands of miles away, on California Avenue in Palo Alto, sheer khurma on Chand Raat is an annual Zareen's tradition.

Unlike our other dessert recipes, this sheer khurma recipe serves a large crowd. For a less ambitious meal, you can halve all the measurements. Sheer khurma keeps well in the fridge in an airtight container for two to three days.

▾▾▾▾▾▾▾▾▾▾▾▾▾▾▾▾▾▾▾▾▾▾▾▾

- In a medium skillet, pan-fry the almonds, pistachios, and raisins in the butter over low heat until golden, 2 to 4 minutes. Use a slotted spoon to remove the nuts and raisins from the butter and set aside. Reserve 3 tablespoons of the fried nut and raisin mix for garnish.

- In a large, heavy-bottomed pot over medium heat, bring the milk to a boil, then reduce the heat to low and slow-cook for 30 to 45 minutes, letting the milk sugars caramelize, until the milk turns a creamy beige color.

- Add the vermicelli to the milk. Increase the heat to medium to bring to a gentle boil before lowering heat down to low-medium. Continue to cook for 15 to 20 minutes, stirring occasionally, until the mixture reaches the consistency of a creamy bisque.

- Once the pudding is at the desired consistency, add in the condensed milk and stir.

- Taste the pudding and add sugar if more sweetness is desired.

- Add the cardamom, pandan flower water, and the butter-fried nuts and raisins. Stir and let simmer for a few more minutes.

- Sheer khurma can be served hot off the stove or stored in the fridge and served cold. We prefer ours nice and warm, and garnished with the butter-fried nuts and raisins kept in reserve.

BESAN-CASHEW BURFI Ⓥ

Gram Flour and Cashew Fudge

¾ cup ghee, or 1½ sticks
  unsalted butter

1 cup gram flour (besan)

1 cup sugar

¼ teaspoon (about 3 pinches)
  ground cardamom

¼ cup raw cashews, chopped

2 tablespoons finely
  chopped raw pistachios

Burfi is Pakistan's take on fudge, and Pakistani fudge can have a dizzying combination of ingredients and flavors. Ours simplifies things with a besan gram flour base and cashew nuts as the primary flavor. Sinfully rich does not begin to describe it. Whether the devil wears Prada or Bata, this is the devil's own dessert. Resistance, dear angel, is futile.

▼▼▼▼▼▼▼▼▼▼▼▼▼▼▼▼▼▼▼▼▼▼▼▼▼▼▼▼

- In a wide pan with a thick base, heat the ghee over medium-low heat. Add the flour and fry until it turns golden pink and fragrant, about 6 to 8 minutes.

- Add in the sugar and cardamom and fry for another 5 minutes. Don't let the flour turn too dark; aim for a golden yellow-brown. A chocolate-brown tinge means it is too dark and will taste burnt.

- Add in the cashews, stir well, and turn off the heat.

- Pour into a 2-quart casserole dish (8-by-6 or 7-by-7 in size), and smooth out and spread with a spoon to get a ¾-inch height. Garnish with the pistachios.

- Let it cool on the counter. Once the fudge cools downs and hardens somewhat, cut it into 16 to 20 1-inch squares.

- Tightly cover the dish with plastic wrap and keep it in the fridge for about 1 hour to cool and harden further, making it easier to remove the pieces from the pan.

- Serve as individual squares arranged on a platter.

CARDAMOM TIRAMISU ⓥ

For the espresso syrup:
5 teaspoons instant espresso powder
2½ cups hot water
¼ cup Torani Amaretto Syrup

For the mascarpone crème:
2 cups heavy cream, chilled
6 tablespoons powdered sugar
1½ teaspoons vanilla extract
2 (8-ounce) tubs mascarpone cheese, at room temperature
30 to 35 Italian ladyfingers *Savoiardi*
⅓ cup Nutella, softened optional
2 biscotti, crushed (optional)
2 teaspoons cocoa powder or shaved hazelnut chocolate

PRO TIPS

It is important that all ingredients excluding the heavy cream are at room temperature, otherwise the dessert may be lumpy or runny.

The ladyfingers should be a little firm, not soggy, after you dip them (don't worry, they will become soft as the dessert sets).

If you like a stronger coffee taste, add an additional 1 tablespoon or so of coffee syrup to the mascarpone crème.

Make sure you wrap your bowl tightly with plastic wrap so it doesn't absorb any odors from the fridge.

Time for our favorite Euro-Pak fusion dessert! This cardamom-infused, egg-free, and marsala wine-free version of the quintessential Italian dessert is a less involved and fully halal adaptation of the Italian classic—but remains sinfully delicious.

▾▾▾▾▾▾▾▾▾▾▾▾▾▾▾▾▾▾▾▾▾▾▾▾▾▾

MAKE THE ESPRESSO SYRUP:

- In a shallow bowl, stir the espresso powder in hot water to dissolve. Let the mixture cool to room temperature.
- Mix in the amaretto syrup and set aside.

MAKE THE MASCARPONE CRÈME:

- In a large bowl using an electric hand mixer, beat the heavy cream until soft peaks form.
- Add in the sugar and vanilla extract, and mix lightly. Don't overbeat!
- In a separate medium bowl, whisk the mascarpone cheese until soft and fluffy. Gently fold it into the whipped cream to ensure an airy batter. Don't overmix!

TO ASSEMBLE:

- Working with 1 ladyfinger at a time, hold at the middle and dip each side quickly in the espresso syrup. The cookie should have a small, hard unsoaked center. Line a glass pan or trifle bowl with these ladyfingers.
- Top this layer of ladyfingers with one third of the mascarpone crème and 2 tablespoons of Nutella.
- Repeat to add a second layer of ladyfingers, mascarpone crème, and Nutella topping.
- Mix the remaining crème with the biscotti. Top the third and final layer of ladyfingers with this biscotti crème and 1 more tablespoon of Nutella.
- Plastic-wrap the container tightly and chill in the fridge for 3 hours, preferably overnight.
- Before serving, sprinkle generously with cocoa powder.

ZAFRANI CARAMEL CUSTARD ⓥ

Crème Caramel with Saffron

1 cup sugar

6 eggs

2 (13-ounce) cans evaporated milk

1 (14-ounce) can condensed milk

1 tablespoon orange zest

1½ teaspoons vanilla extract

1 teaspoon of saffron strands

Hot water, for water bath

Crème caramel or caramel custard is one of the most popular western desserts in Pakistan, routinely gracing the menus of upscale restaurants, cafés, and country clubs. Our recipe upgrades these childhood memories by adding zafran saffron. For best results, use a 1½-quart flan pan, measuring 6 to 8 inches in diameter.

▾▾▾▾▾▾▾▾▾▾▾▾▾▾▾▾▾▾▾▾▾▾▾▾▾▾

◆ Preheat the oven to 350 degrees F.

◆ In a medium-size flan pan, heat the sugar over medium heat.

◆ Constantly stir the sugar until it becomes candy clear and then turns golden brown, 6 to 8 minutes. Don't let it become dark brown. Tilt the pan to swirl the caramel around the sides. Remove from heat.

◆ In a large bowl, whisk the eggs together. Mix in the evaporated milk and condensed milk, and whisk together. Then add the orange zest, vanilla extract, and saffron, and whisk until smooth.

◆ Pour the custard into the caramel-lined flan pan. Place the flan pan in a larger pan and pour 1 to 2 inches of hot water in the large pan surrounding the custard pan.

◆ Bake for 50 to 60 minutes in the water bath and check with a knife just to the side of the center. If the knife comes out clean, the custard is ready.

◆ Let it cool in the fridge for at least 1 hour.

◆ To serve, run a knife around the edges to loosen and invert onto a serving plate.

STACY BROWN-PHILPOT

Business Leader

WHY WE LOVE STACY

We love all our loyal patrons at Zareen's, but we don't always think of them whenever we go shopping at Nordstrom, or find help on TaskRabbit, or print out our Women's Day flyers on our HP printer. Unless they happen to be Stacy Brown-Philpot, the former CEO of TaskRabbit, former senior director at Google, and board member at HP and Nordstrom! From investing in Black and Latine entrepreneurs at Cherryrock Capital, to serving on the board of Black Girls Code, Stacy is a mentor and inspiration to the next generation of minorities and women everywhere, including at home to her daughters.

CHOSEN CHARITY: PLANNED PARENTHOOD

When we asked Stacy to choose a charity to support through the sale of this book, she picked Planned Parenthood, which has advocated for the protection of reproductive rights and has provided reproductive and sexual healthcare in the United States since 1916. Each year, Planned Parenthood delivers sexual and reproductive healthcare and information to millions of people in the United States.

STACY'S MESSAGE: BE WILLING TO ASK FOR WHAT YOU NEED

"Back in 2009, I had just moved into a new role at Google when I was asked if I wanted to go to India to head our sales operations. This meant living apart from my husband for a whole year, delaying our plans to start a family, and living and working in a new country by myself. But the more I thought about it, the more I wanted to take this on. So I wrote down what I and my family needed to make this happen and then I asked my manager for it. He agreed. Just a few weeks later, I was on my way to India. Looking back, I wouldn't change that decision for anything. You should never be afraid to ask for what you need to make your whole life—not just your work life—work for you."

A FAVORITE EAT: GRANDMA'S LEMON POUND CAKE

Stacy told us that this lemon pound cake recipe was handed down to her by her grandmother and has been dutifully passed on by her to her daughters. Like most beloved family recipes, its ingredients are imprecisely measured. And it is this imprecision that makes it perfect:

Sift about 3 cups of flour and ½ teaspoon of baking powder into a bowl, and set this dry mix aside. Cream 1 cup of butter and about ½ cup of shortening together using an electric mixer. Gradually add 3 cups of sugar while beating until it's light and fluffy. Add 6 eggs, one at a time, beating well after each addition. Add about 1 teaspoon each of lemon extract and vanilla extract. Mix well. Now add the dry ingredients into the batter alternating with 1 cup of milk. Mix well and your batter is ready.

Spoon this batter into a greased 10-inch tube cake pan. Place in a cold oven and bake at 350 degrees F for 1½ hours or until done. Cool before serving.

SOOJI HALWA ⓥ

Sweet Semolina Confection with Cardamom

¾ cup ghee

2 cardamom pods

1 cup (240 g) semolina flour

2 cups sugar

½ teaspoon saffron (optional)

Dash of yellow food coloring (optional)

1 tablespoon slivered almonds (optional)

1 tablespoon chopped unsalted raw pistachios (optional)

PRO TIP

Like others in the halwa family, sooji halwa stores well when refrigerated, easily keeping for 3 to 4 days. Always reheat the portion you need on a frying pan before serving.

Halwa or halva is a traditional South Asian and Middle Eastern confection consisting of flour, sugar, nuts, and various flavors and essences, all fried in butter or ghee. In Pakistan, sooji semolina flour halwa is especially popular as it is the main sweet component of the popular brunch Halwa Puri Nashta (page 87), served with puris, cholay, and aloo bhujia.

Easy to prepare, sooji halwa is the perfect way to make family members feel special with an after-meal treat, to please invited guests at a dinner party, or to play gracious, unperturbed host to unexpected guests. With our recipe, and a bit of practice, you should be able to perform alchemy on sugar, ghee, and water to give your sooji halwa an unctuous, almost gluey consistency.

▾▾▾▾▾▾▾▾▾▾▾▾▾▾▾▾▾▾▾▾▾▾▾▾▾▾▾▾

- In a Dutch oven or large pot, heat the ghee over medium heat, then add the cardamom and stir for a few seconds. Add the flour and stir over medium-low heat until the flour turns light pink in color, 3 to 5 minutes.

- Add in the sugar, 2½ cups of water, the saffron, and yellow food coloring. Turn the heat up to medium. Stir consistently until the halwa thickens, 6 to 8 minutes.

- Cover and leave on low heat for another 5 to 7 minutes until the oil separates. Your halwa should glisten and reach an unctuous, slightly sticky consistency.

- Ladle the halwa onto a dessert platter and top with the almonds and pistachios. Serve hot.

ROSE ICE CREAM ⓥ

1 (14-ounce) can sweet-
   ened condensed milk
1 (12-ounce) can
   evaporated milk
2 cups (16 ounces)
   heavy cream
¼ cup chopped raw
   pistachios plus
   1 tablespoon, divided
2 to 3 tablespoons rose
   syrup (we prefer Rooz
   Afza), plus more for garnish
2 tablespoons rose
   preserves (we prefer
   Ahmed Foods), optional
¼ teaspoon ground
   cardamom
1 cup Cool Whip whipped
   topping

PRO TIP

If you want a deeper pink
color, add 2 drops of
red food coloring to the
milk and essence mixture
before blending.

A quick and easy, no machines, no hand-churning required ice cream, this rose flavored frozen dessert is sure to be an instant hit at home. Rose syrup, rose preserves, cardamom, and pistachios give a Desi stamp to this delicious dessert.

▼▼▼▼▼▼▼▼▼▼▼▼▼▼▼▼▼▼▼▼▼▼▼▼▼

- In a blender, add the condensed milk, evaporated milk, cream, ¼ cup of pistachios, 2 tablespoon rose syrup, rose preserves, and cardamom, and blend until all the ingredients are well combined.

- Gently fold in the Cool Whip topping. Taste, and add more rose syrup if desired.

- Pour the mixture into small, 4-ounce plastic Dixie cups—you should have enough for 8 to 10 cups.

- Garnish each cup with a sprinkle of chopped pistachios from the remaining 1 tablespoon and a few drops of rose syrup.

- Cover with aluminum foil and freeze for at least 5 hours.

- Serve in individual dessert bowls.

ON KULFI

The heat of the subcontinental summer cannot be subdued by mere ice cream. Creamier, denser, colder, kulfi is the superhero dessert we Pakistanis need and deserve.

Its cardamom-scented flesh is more taut than any ice cream's. As you bite into its sweet glacial mass, there is a barely perceptible graininess, which would be the ruin of any ice cream but is the hallmark of great kulfi.

Kulfi is traditionally served as a conical frustum in a pool of caramelized milk. Amid the heat of summer days and our lascivious gaze, our kulfi may start to melt; but as it merely trickles into the creamy pond below, no goodness is ever lost. This feature is not available in the mobile version—a more slender cone skewered on a stick—which must be nibbled and slurped more greedily. This is a happy requirement.

There is malai cream kulfi and there is pista pistachio kulfi: there are no other morally acceptable versions. The only admissible variation is to pair kulfi with the dessert drink Falooda (page 227), a gastronomical theme park of rose-infused cream-milk, with chunks of jelly, slippery glass noodles, and sweet basil seeds. Even purists grudgingly accept the falooda's vibrant colors and textures as worthy additions.

The kulfi beginner can, after much comparative study, choose to be conservative kulfi, neat or progressive kulfi falooda. Or they may remain, like many of us, happily independent.

KULFI

Traditional Pakistani Ice Cream

Perhaps the most popular of all South Asian desserts, kulfi has never been so easy to make! As with our rose ice cream recipe, there is no need for machines, nor for hand-churning. You can use popsicle molds steel or silicone or small Dixie cups to freeze and serve kulfi.

1 (14-ounce) can condensed milk

1 (12-ounce) can evaporated milk

1 (8-ounce) carton heavy cream

½ cup raw shelled pistachios

½ teaspoon ground cardamom

2 white bread slices

PISTA KULFI ⓥ

Pistachio Ice Cream

In our instant adaptation of this frozen dessert, cardamom-infused cream and milk are flavored with crushed raw pistachios for pista kulfi, the original and still the best kulfi.

▼▼▼▼▼▼▼▼▼▼▼▼▼▼▼▼▼▼▼▼▼▼▼▼▼▼▼▼

- In a blender, blend all the ingredients until smooth.
- Pour the blended mixture into popsicle molds or small, 4-ounce Dixie cups.
- Freeze for at least 5 hours.
- To serve, take the kulfi out of the molds or cups and place in a saucer or bowl for a few minutes so that the kulfi becomes slightly pliable (no longer frozen hard) and is easily cut through with a spoon.

MANGO KULFI ⓥ
Mango Ice Cream

1 (14-ounce) can
  condensed milk
1 (12-ounce) can
  evaporated milk
1 (8-ounce) carton
  heavy cream
1½ cups canned
  mango pulp
2 tablespoons sugar
¼ teaspoon ground
  green cardamom

PRO TIP

Note the absence of bread
slices in mango kulfi; the
mango pulp used here
provides the texture that
we create with bread in the
pistachio kulfi recipe.

We purists who grew up on the pistachio kulfi have grudgingly also fallen for mango kulfi, which has taken newer generations of Pakistanis by storm and may well be the most popular flavor among the South Asian diaspora and their friends. And so we also include here a mango kulfi recipe, in which cardamom-infused milk and cream are flavored with mango pulp, chilled, and served. The directions for this recipe are the same as for pista kulfi; simply use the ingredients below instead.

▾▾▾▾▾▾▾▾▾▾▾▾▾▾▾▾▾▾▾▾▾▾▾▾▾▾▾

- In a blender, blend all the ingredients until smooth.
- Pour the blended mixture into popsicle molds or small, 4-ounce Dixie cups.
- Freeze for at least 5 hours.
- To serve, take the kulfi out of the molds or cups and place in a saucer or bowl for a few minutes so that the kulfi becomes slightly pliable (no longer frozen hard) and is easily cut through with a spoon

Menu Planning

Here are some menu suggestions that will help you wow family, friends, colleagues, and special someones alike. We start with quick and easy weeknight dinners, move to more elaborate meals and dinner party menus, and finally to special occasion dinners. A few notes:

- You'll find information about any recommended accompaniments kachumar, raita, and chutneys in the main dish recipes—many of these can be made ahead of time.

- You can get store-bought or restaurant-made parathas and naans to simplify your prep work.

- Pakistani meals don't feature salads prominently, but feel free to add your favorite salad at the top of the menu.

- All good Pakistani meals are usually rounded out with a cup of chai. Add regular chai black tea with milk, Doodh Patti Chai (page 225), or Kashmiri Chai (page 222) to any menu.

MIX-AND-MATCH WEEKNIGHT MEALS

Combine the easiest of our meat and vegetarian main dishes with a lentil dish and rice or bread of your choice for busy weeknights. Don't forget to add the usual accompaniments!

CHOOSE A MEAT MAIN: Aloo Qeema (page 121), Chapli Kabab (page 129), or Laal Masala Fish (page 143)

CHOOSE A VEGGIE DISH: Turai Sabzi (page 146), Bhindi Masala (page 157), or Aloo Palak (page 147)

CHOOSE A LENTIL: Tarka Daal (page 159), Kaali Masoor ki Daal (page 160), or Lahori Cholay (page 162)

CHOOSE RICE OR BREAD: Plain White Basmati Rice (page 168) or Roti (page 181)

WEEKEND MEALS

More time to cook means slightly more elaborate menus. To each of the following signature mains, add a lentil dish, such as Tarka Daal (page 159), Kaali Masoor ki Daal (page 160), or Lahori Cholay (page 162), and a rice pudding, such as Kheer (page 230) or Firni (page 230), or a dessert drink, such as Mango Lassi or Rose Lassi (page 218).

BEEF: Aloo Gosht (page 120) with Matar Pulao (page 172)

CHICKEN: Memoni Crispy Fried Chicken (page 95) with Karachi-Style Coleslaw (page 209) and Baked Masala Potato Wedges (page 74)

VEGETARIAN: Madras Coconut Curry with Paneer and Vegetables (page 106) with Aloo Tikki (page 151) and Aromatic Yellow Rice (page 170)

SUNDAY BRUNCH

Protein Power Brunch

Khageena (page 83) or Masala Omelet (page 82)

Muttar Qeema (page 121)

Laal Masala Aloo (page 153)

Memoni Carrot Achar (page 212)

CHOOSE: Lachha Paratha (page 189), regular Paratha (page 184), Roti (page 181), or toasted bread

Doodh Patti Chai (page 225)

Vegetarian Brunch

Halwa Puri Nashta (page 87)

Doodh Patti Chai (page 225)

DINNER PARTIES

Meat Lover's Gala

Memoni Samosa (page 58) or Bun Kabab (page 70)

Kofta Saalan (page 122), Karahi Chicken (page 94), or Memoni Coconut Shrimp Curry (page 142)

Memoni Crispy Fried Lamb Chops with Mashed Potato Crust (page 130)

Aromatic Yellow Rice (page 170)

Tarka Daal (page 159)

Naan (page 193)

Zafrani Caramel Custard (page 238)

Vegan Soiree

Aloo Pakora and Eggplant Pakoras (page 55)

Coconut Chickpea Curry (page 164)

Bhindi Masala (page 157) made with oil

Kaali Masoor ki Daal (page 160) made with oil

Zeera Aloo (page 154) made with oil

Paratha (page 184) and/or Roti (page 181) made with oil

Sooji Halwa (page 241) made with oil instead of ghee

VALENTINE'S DAY DINNER

Here are two suggestions for a romantic dinner.

The Quickie

Desi Paleo Salad (page 66)

Laal Masala Fish (page 143)

Bhindi Masala (page 157)

Matar Pulao (page 172)

Rose Ice Cream (page 243)

The Labor of Love

Memoni Samosa (page 58)

Memoni Crispy Fried Lamb Chops with Mashed Potato Crust (page 130)

Madras Coconut Curry with Chicken (page 106)

Saffron and Butter Rice with Cashews and Cranberries (page 171)

Cardamom Tiramisu (page 237)

EID FEAST

All suggested Eid menu items are subject to change by you—except sheer khurma.

Memoni Samosa (page 58)

Dahi Baray (page 61)

Chicken Pulao (page 174), Karachi Biryani (page 178), or Chicken Haleem (page 102)

Gola Kabab (page 126) or Grilled Chicken Boti (page 99)

Lahori Cholay (page 162)

Laal Masala Aloo (page 153)

Naan (page 193) and regular Paratha (page 184)

Sheer Khurma (page 233)

Sooji Halwa (page 241)

DIWALI BANQUET

A vegetarian spread that will set your guests aglow on the festival of lights.

Onion Pakora (page 54)

Roasted Eggplant Yogurt (page 161)

Palak Paneer (page 148)

Coconut Chickpea Curry (page 164)

Bhindi Masala (page 157)

Saffron and Butter Rice with Cashews and Cranberries (page 171)

Garlic Naan (page 193) and Paratha (page 184)

Besan-Cashew Burfi (page 234)

Kheer (page 230)

SUMMER BARBECUE

Choose one (or both!) of our suggested build-your-own themes.

Build-Your-Own Desi Burgers

Chapli Kabab (page 129) or vegetarian option, Aloo Tikki (page 151)

Assorted grilled vegetables

Assorted Toppings: lettuce, onions, tomatoes, and pickles

Garlic-Chili Ketchup (page 207) and/or Hari Chutney (page 205)

Hamburger buns

Build-Your-Own Desi Fajitas

Grilled Chicken Boti (page 99) or vegetarian option, Zeera Aloo (page 154)

Kachumar (page 208)

Wicked Spicy Chutney (page 207)

Tortillas or Paratha (page 184)

To either, add:

Fruit Chaat (page 64)

Roasted Eggplant Yogurt (page 161)

Masala Fries (page 75)

Karachi-Style Coleslaw (page 209)

Mango Kulfi (page 247)

HOLIDAY DINNERS

Replace or augment your usual Thanksgiving and Christmas mains and sides with these Pakistani counterparts.

SOUP: Yakhni (page 79)

ROAST: Pomegranate-Garlic Roast Chicken with Gravy (page 114)

LAMB: Memoni Crispy Fried Lamb Chops with Mashed Potato Crust (page 130)

POTATOES: Laal Masala Aloo (page 153) or Baked Masala Potato Wedges (page 74)

BEANS/LENTILS: Kaali Masoor ki Daal (page 160)

RICE: Matar Pulao (page 172) or Saffron and Butter Rice with Cashews and Cranberries (page 171)

DIPS AND SIDES: Roasted Eggplant Yogurt (page 161), Beet Raita (page 203), or Karachi-Style Coleslaw (page 209)

DESSERT: Zafrani Caramel Custard (page 238) or Kheer (page 230)

PARTING

THOUGHTS

Recommended Reading

Every Zareen's restaurant features a wall of hanging books, with all volumes donated from our home library. Following in that tradition, here are some of our favorite fiction and nonfiction books about Pakistan.

A Case of Exploding Mangoes, MOHAMMED HANIF
Possibly the most entertaining and certainly the most irreverent book on our list, and that's saying something for a list that includes *Moth Smoke* and *The Crow Eaters*, Mohammed Hanif's side-splitting account of mile-high assassinations and military amours is the fitting mic-drop end to our list.

The Crow Eaters, BAPSI SIDHWA
The debut novel from the queen of Pakistani fiction, *The Crow Eaters* is a loving, laugh-out-loud look at the Parsi community living out their lives in the vanity fair of Lahore society. Relish this short novel slowly to stay the inevitable disappointment of finishing a great book.

In Other Rooms, Other Wonders, DANIYAL MUEENUDDIN
You had us at the title. It is a wonder that the stories actually live up to their collective name. Unflinchingly humane, these would have been the tales Chekhov would have told, had he lived in Pakistan instead of Russia.

Instant City: Life and Death in Karachi, STEVE INSKEEP
In unfolding the tale of a single harrowing day, Steve Inskeep unravels the timeless hopes and history of Karachi's twenty million citizens.

Karachi, You're Killing Me!, SABA IMTIAZ

We are suckers for this witty, fast-paced thriller and comedy of manners narrated by an attractive journalist in search of love and a good hair day. This one is possibly more endearing than Bridget Jones and based in our favorite city, Karachi.

Kartography, KAMILA SHAMSIE

This novel is a beautifully crafted and surprisingly humorous map of an upper-class Karachi childhood, skeletons in a Pakistani family closet, love in the time of urban warfare, and the civil war that tore up our country.

Lahore by Metro, FAIZAN AHMAD

Faizan Ahmad's pictorial and verbal stories of everyday folks turn the daily lives of the humans of Lahore into high art. It is the art gallery and contemporary history museum that Lahore deserves.

Moth Smoke, MOHSIN HAMID

A personal favorite, a national treasure, a murder mystery, and a love story, *Moth Smoke* is the one true anthem of the operatic trainwreck that is Karachi society.

Pakistan: A Hard Country, ANATOL LIEVEN

An investigative journalist, a policy analyst, and a trained anthropologist set out to investigate and ultimately dispel many of the dehumanizing myths and cliches about Pakistan. Read this brilliant book and you will see that he succeeds.

In Gratitude

We must begin by thanking you, dear reader, for picking up this book, and it seems, reading it cover to cover. We hope you have enjoyed reading and using it as much as we have writing it for you. Thank you for spreading the joy of Pakistani cooking and supporting our mission of women empowerment.

We thank all the patrons of Zareen's restaurant, without who's support even the notion of this book would not exist. A double thanks to those of you who are both customers and readers. We are deeply grateful to the dedication and endless stamina of our team: to everyone who is or has been part of Zareen's restaurant, including (and especially) our son Sahlik, who is now part of the Zareen's team and of the journey to come.

This cookbook would not have been possible without three sets of remarkable women. We will start by thanking its first champion in the publishing world: our agent Stacey Glick (of Dystel Goderich & Bourret), who evangelized this project to publishers across America. Profound thanks also to our editor Hannah Elnan for being a most patient coach and guide through this process (and the best of recipe testers!); art director Anna Goldstein for her unerring eye for visual magic; managing editor Peggy Gannon for shepherding the book through to launch; and Jill Saginario, the first person to support this project at Sasquatch Books, and who returned to guide us across the finish line. By extension, we are grateful to Sasquatch for putting their faith in a book about Karachi childhoods and Pakistani recipes.

Next, our special thanks to the women who made this book the visual feast it is: Neetu Laddha and her genius for photographic storytelling (and for being a huge Zareen's fan!); Yasna Glumac for her food styling and calm amid creative storm; Eemaan Bano Rahman (of Beygumbano fame) for vividly stroking out our entire culinary past and present on a 7 ¼-by-10-inch book cover; and Khaula Jamil for snapping joyous moments from our beloved Karachi for our book.

Much gratitude is also due to a third set of remarkable women: the trailblazers who are spotlighted in this book. Rupi, Nadiya, Stacy, Sana, Michelle, and Ayesha: thank you for agreeing so graciously and promptly to be part of this project, for sharing your passions and messages with our readers, and for gracing our pages with the beauty of your person and your craft.

We thank our family of friends, here in America and back in Pakistan, for everything from last-minute jars of saffron needed for photo shoots (thank you, Fariha!), to kitchen testing many of the recipes, to cheering our every step on this book's journey—and the entirety of Zareen's journey. Special thanks to our friends Sameen and Abid of Nani Khatai and Shiza Shahid of Our Place cookware for sustaining our cooking (and eating) needs with their products and goodwill. We are blessed that we have too many friends to mention all by name here, given the constraints of modern publishing and tyrannies of page count economics.

We owe our well-fed childhoods and our well-nourished lives to the love and support of our families and friends: to our parents, present in our lives or ever-present in our memories; to our dear children, Samar, Sahlik, and Amara; to our sisters, Shazaf and Parveen (forever our biggest champions), and their families; to our nieces and nephews and uncles and aunts—including and especially all aunts bonded not by blood but by heart. And so, like blades of grass repaying the warmth of the summer sun, we thank them. Above all else, we thank them.

Index

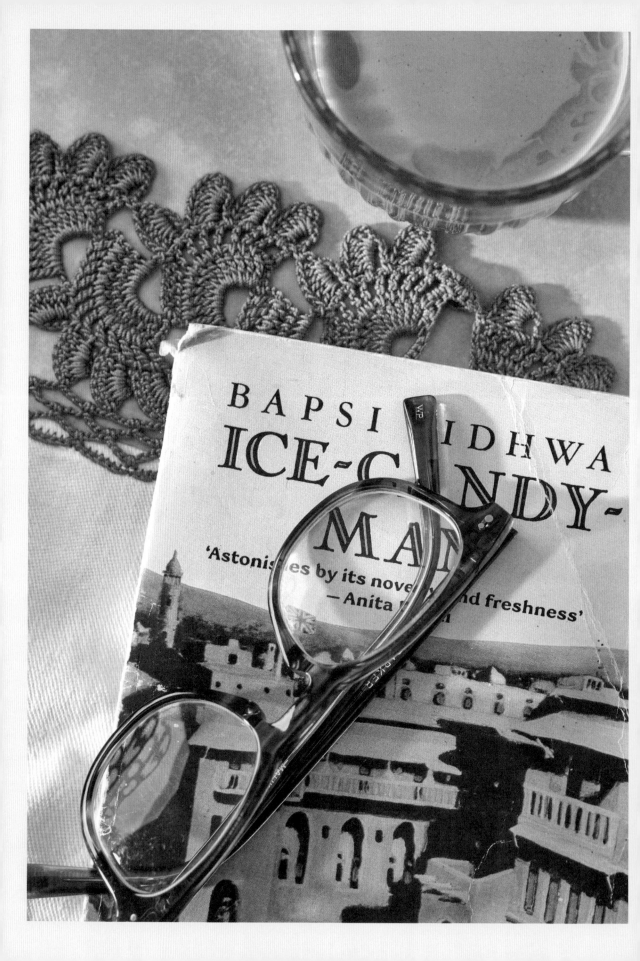

Conversions

VOLUME

UNITED STATES	METRIC	IMPERIAL
¼ tsp.	1.25 mL	
½ tsp.	2.5 mL	
1 tsp.	5 mL	
½ Tbsp.	7.5 mL	
1 Tbsp.	15 mL	
⅛ c.	30 mL	1 fl. oz.
¼ c.	60 mL	2 fl. oz.
⅓ c.	80 mL	2.5 fl. oz.
½ c.	120 mL	4 fl. oz.
1 c.	230 mL	8 fl. oz.
2 c. (1 pt.)	460 mL	16 fl. oz.
1 qt.	1 L	32 fl. oz.

LENGTH

UNITED STATES	METRIC
⅛ in.	3 mm
¼ in.	6 mm
½ in.	1.25 cm
1 in.	2.5 cm
1 ft.	30 cm

WEIGHT

AVOIRDUPOIS	METRIC
¼ oz.	7 g
½ oz.	15 g
1 oz.	30 g
2 oz.	60 g
3 oz.	90 g
4 oz.	115 g
5 oz.	150 g
6 oz.	175 g
7 oz.	200 g
8 oz. (½ lb.)	225 g
9 oz.	250 g
10 oz.	300 g
11 oz.	325 g
12 oz.	350 g
13 oz.	375 g
14 oz.	400 g
15 oz.	425 g
16 oz. (1 lb.)	450 g
1½ lb.	750 g
2 lb.	900 g
2¼ lb.	1 kg
3 lb.	1.4 kg
4 lb.	1.8 kg

TEMPERATURE

OVEN MARK	FAHRENHEIT	CELSIUS	GAS
Very cool	250–275	120–135	½–1
Cool	300	150	2
Warm	325	165	3
Moderate	350	175	4
Moderately hot	375	190	5
Fairly hot	400	200	6
Hot	425	220	7
Very hot	450	230	8
Very hot	475	245	9

For ease of use, conversions have been rounded.

SNAPSHOTS FROM
WELL-FED CHILDHOODS

About the Authors

ZAREEN KHAN

Though Zareen's family hails from Bombay, India, Zareen was born in Karachi, Pakistan. She is a Northeastern graduate who left her corporate career to start her food business in 2009. Hugely popular cooking classes led to her iconic namesake restaurant. She specializes in Pakistani and North Indian food while celebrating the cuisine of the Memons, an ethnic community from Gujarat India and Karachi, to which her family belongs. Zareen started her restaurant business at forty-three, shortly after winning her battle with oral cancer in 2012. Now a celebrated restaurateur, Zareen has a global following for her eponymous restaurants with three Bay Area locations and more planned. She has been covered in numerous print, online, and TV media outlets including PBS, NPR, Fox News, the *San Francisco Chronicle*, and the *Mercury News*, and was profiled in *The Immigrant Cookbook* by Leyla Moushabeck alongside renowned chefs Iván Garcia, José Andrés, and Daniel Boulud.

UMAIR KHAN

Also born in Karachi, Pakistan, Umair graduated from MIT where he majored in mathematics with a humanities concentration in writing. He is a visiting professor at University of California, Berkeley, where he teaches "HUM 120: Entrepreneurship for All," in the College of Letters & Science. He is the author of *College Application Hacked* and regularly conducts workshops on college admissions. Besides cofounding Zareen's with his wife, Umair is the founder of Folio3, a global tech services firm, and a founding partner at Mentors Fund, an early-stage tech investment firm.

Contributors

NEETU LADDHA
FOOD PHOTOGRAPHER

Raised in Rajasthan (India) and now based in San Francisco, Neetu Laddha blends her culinary background with her passion for photography. Her organic style, influenced by her upbringing, uses bright colors and lived-in photography to create vibrant, joyful images that perfectly match Zareen's essence. Each photo captures the warmth and richness of her cultural heritage, making the dishes come alive on the pages.

KHAULA JAMIL
KARACHI PHOTOGRAPHER

Born and raised in Karachi, Khuala Jamil is an independent freelance documentary photographer, photojournalist, and filmmaker. She covers diverse subjects ranging from climate change and health to agriculture and human rights all over Pakistan.

EEMAAN BANO RAHMAN
COVER ARTIST

Eemaan Bano Rahman, better known by her alias Beygumbano, is an artist and designer based in Pakistan and Dubai. Her work takes inspiration from the whimsical in the worldly and the mundane in the fantastical. Her philosophy is shaped by her love for daydreaming and storytelling that is often inspired by subcontinental history and social structures, filtered by a lens of hide and seek, irreverent romanticism and nostalgia.

Printed in China

SASQUATCH BOOKS with colophon is a registered trademark of Blue Star Press, LLC

29 28 27 26 25   9 8 7 6 5 4 3 2 1

Editors: Hannah Elnan and Jill Saginario
Production editor: Peggy Gannon / Cover art: Beygumbano
Designer: Anna Goldstein / Food photography: Neetu Laddha
Food styling: Yasna Glumac / Karachi photography: Khaula Jamil
Family portrait (page 284, top left): Mark Tuschman
Other family photos courtesy of Zareen and Umair Khan

Spotlight photos: Nadiya Hussain by Anne Kibel (page 65); Sana Amanat by Judy Stephens (page 71); Ayesha Chundrigar by Ayesha Chundrigar (page 165); Michelle Tam by Henry Fong (page 187); Rupi Kaur by Baljit Singh (page 223); Stacy Brown-Philpot by Ricardo Téllez (page 240)

Page iv, poem reproduced by permission from Rupi Kaur

Library of Congress Cataloging-in-Publication Data
Names: Khan, Umair (Umair Azim), author. | Khan, Zareen, author.
Title: Zareen's Pakistani kitchen : Recipes from a well-fed childhood written by Umair Khan ; recipes by Zareen Khan.
Description: Seattle : Sasquatch Books, [2025] Includes index
Identifiers: LCCN 2024027347 | ISBN 9781632175298 (hardcover) | ISBN 9781632175304 (epub)
Subjects: LCSH: Cooking, Pakistani
Classification: LCC TX724.5.P3 K43 2025 | DDC 641.595491--dc23/eng/20240809
LC record available at https://lccn.loc.gov/2024027347

ISBN: 978-1-63217-529-8

Sasquatch Books
1325 Fourth Avenue, Suite 1025
Seattle, WA 98101

SasquatchBooks.com